Solving the Puzzles of Life

Kyle Shiver

Copyright © 2015 Kyle Shiver

All rights reserved.

ISBN: 1515350649
ISBN-13:978-151535-0644

DEDICATION

This book is dedicated to my wife and daughter, Heather and Lily, both of whom I love more than love itself. (Bigger than the sky.)

If tomorrow is judgment day (Sing Mommy)
And I'm standing on the front line
And the Lord asks me what I did with my life
I will say I spent it with you

Songwriters
Duplessis, Jerry / Jean, Wyclef
Performed by Whitney Houston

CONTENTS

	Acknowledgments	i
	Introduction	viii
	Personal Testimony	xi
1	The Technique	1
2	Knowing That You Know	4
3	How We Communicate With The Universe	10
4	Universal Access	17
5	Your New Life	23
6	It's Nothing Personal	27
7	Anything Really Is Possible!	31
8	An Orderly Process	34
9	Change The Question	37
10	Changing the Associations	46
11	The Most Subtle Thought	57
12	The Responsibility Clause	59
13	The Thing We Want The Most	68
14	And So It Already Is!	73
	Appendix	77

ACKNOWLEDGMENTS

Having been introduced to the world of spirituality back in the mid-eighties, you could conclude that every person and every aspect of life since then has been in some way an integral part of my journey.

My teachers who have transitioned are Jesus, Buddha, Lao-Tzu, and from more recent years, Paramahansa Yogananda, OSHO, Charles and Myrtle Fillmore, Ernest Holmes, and Joel Goldsmith.

There are many teachers living in modern day that I've not met, but should undoubtedly thank, such as Master Eckhart Tolle, Don Miguel Ruiz, Gary Bernard, Louise Hay, Tania Kotsos, Deepak Chopra, Thich Nhat Hanh, and his holiness the Dalai Lama.

Then there are those living whom I have the pleasure of speaking with and working with, and learning from first-hand, such as Susan Boles, Jennye Johnson, and Dave Arsenaulk.

To my mentor the Reverend Dale Worley, who has been so instrumental in much of my spiritual development these past few years. Thank you for setting such a good example for us all, and for being my doorway into this new and beautiful world.

I thank my mother and father who have been there at each step along the way to support me, even though at times I am sure they were wondering, "What planet is this kid from?" Without their dedication and love I may easily have left this world a long time ago, never having seen and experienced the beauty that I have seen and that I experience today.

And to my lovely wife Heather, who always has been and always will be the only one for me. It just is. She knows me like no one else does. And though she doesn't always agree or understand me, she loves me anyway. Together we were blessed to bring a beautiful daughter into the world, and I would be amiss if I didn't thank her too. Lily is the most beautiful spirit, so full of life.

Even though I am her father, she is quite often my teacher.

I'd also like to thank Angie Celeste, who has been a strong supporter of my ministry, Angie has never failed to donate her time to create logo's, posters and flyers, and now to create this beautiful cover! I am grateful. And thanks to David Smiley for the wonderful sketches!

Others who come to mind are Ryan Sylvester, Russell Swinger, all those I've had the honor of playing music with, the people involved in our spiritual movement Tybee Spirit and who have been of great support to me such as Carol Hodges, Elisabeth Edge, Donna Elliott, Kimberly Carver, Dicky Trotter, and basically anyone and everyone who I come into contact with… thank you!

Last but not least I send thanks to my editor Lesta Sue Hardee, who came in to my life last year, and we have become like brother and sister.

It is amazing how the Universe works to put exactly the right people in your life at exactly the right time, and how we can work together so fluidly.

The fact is that at some point about five years ago now, I just started writing and couldn't stop. This, along with my seeming lack of organizational skills, has created quite a mess. Lesta Sue has just what it takes to get me to cull through and piece together a concise body of work such as this one.

It is as if I brought to her a bag full of wooden blocks with letters on them, and she placed them all together in order, just right. Thank you sister.

To you the reader, there are no mistakes in this Universe and it is no mistake that we should meet here and under these exact circumstances.

It is nice to meet you.

Much love and many blessings on your journey,
Kyle Shiver
June 11th 2015
Savannah GA.

INTRODUCTION

I was in middle school when the Rubik's Cube came out.

It was all the rage.

One morning before school a group of us were standing around passing a cube around and gazing at it. We would each take some turns at it, but we didn't know how to solve it.

A fellow student walked up and saw the cube and said, "Let me see that thing for a minute."

He turned it over a few times, and I could see that he could see.

I could tell that he somehow related to the puzzle and that he would be able to figure it out.

"Can I take this to class and bring it back to you between classes?" he asked.

The kid who owned it said, "Sure!"

Later he brought the cube back and said, "It's easy!"

Well maybe it was easy for him, but the rest of us didn't think so. He tried to explain it to us but we didn't really get it.

In the coming months I saw kids peeling off the stickers and placing them back in order to make each side a solid color. Some of us also figured out how to take the cube apart and then put it back together solved.

There were some kids who knew how to work the puzzle, but the majority of us it seemed, didn't.

I ended up getting a book at the mall that had step-by-step instructions.

By following each step closely, I could solve the puzzle too. But I never really "got it" or related to it.

This is such a perfect example of life and the puzzles of life that we encounter.

Why do some people just naturally know how to work the puzzle, while others have no clue?

You may understand a puzzle that I don't understand, while I may understand a puzzle that you don't understand. You may be really good at drawing and painting, but have no musical talent. I may be exactly the opposite.

It seems that each of us is different and each of us has different talents and understandings. But when it comes to basic life puzzles, does this mean we have to go through life just "not knowing?"

Do I have to go through life never having a good relationship? Addicted to alcohol or some other drug? Do I have to go through life and not be successful? Do I have to go through life not getting what I want? Do I have to go through life not understanding? Not being able to forgive people from my past? Do I have to go through life not understanding the Universe or God?

No you don't.

Whatever puzzle you have in your life it is exactly like the Rubik's Cube. There are people who know how to solve it. There are books to instruct you.

In this book we will talk about going from A to Z one step at a time. We will also talk about the fact that there is no reason to take our life puzzles personally.
The Rubik's Cube is not personal. Buy the book, follow the steps, and the puzzle will be solved. All of our life puzzles are this same way. Impersonal.

Whether you understand the puzzle or not, the moves to solve it are the same.

If you practice the technique I'm going to share with you in this book just a little, you will soon see that it does indeed work.

Instead of trying to move way down the line, just give the instruction, "Bring the next step to me". So instead of
 instructing to finish the puzzle on the next move, which the Universe cannot do, (the masters can work the Rubik's Cube in 20 moves, but they have to take each of the steps) we will learn to solve any puzzle, one step at a time.

You then of course, proceed taking a step at a time, and before you know it, everything in your life will increase.

This technique and the principles I teach are all based in Universal Law, and so cannot fail. You do the moves, and whatever puzzle or challenge you may face, it will be solved.

Out of curiosity, I did some searching around on Google, and asked the question, "How many solutions are there to the Rubik's Cube?" I discovered that they have worked the cube from any point in twenty moves, but also; *"An infinite amount of solutions. Reason why is because you could turn the cube 1,000 times to solve it, or 2,000 times to solve it, or... well, you get my point. If you were looking for Permutations, here's the original answer: There are 43,252,003,274,489,856,000 (43 quintillion, 252 quadrillion, 3 trillion, 274 billion, 489 million, 856 thousand) possible solutions for the cube, but there is only one correct one!"*

It turns out that whatever puzzle we face in life there are more solutions that the mind can imagine.

Each of us has access to these solutions.

PERSONAL TESTIMONY

We all have this innate desire to do something. Once we begin, then we enter into what I believe to be a new state of consciousness. This is a new realm, or plane of existence.

Everything is different for us now.

Yes, there is a path leading to Self-Realization. The time before is usually spent in the not knowing, or living with alcoholism or other addictions.

There are people too, who never really question or seem to have a need for anything other than what they have. I have encountered many people who just naturally understand the order of things and who are in the flow already.

For those of us who are awakening, once it starts, you cannot ever shut it off.

"Why am I here?" "The Universe is so amazing, and I need to know what this is all for." "I feel as if there is something for me to do, but I am not sure what it is."

We must have a purpose or a reason for being here, or … we wouldn't be here.
In my own personal case, there were lots of battles with alcohol and addictions in my very early years, but I got clean at the age of seventeen, and to everyone's amazement, (including my own), I stayed clean.

The days turned into months and the months turned into years, and I managed to kick my alcoholism and addiction problems.

Things were rocky at times, and there were times when it did not seem as if I would be able to hang on. But I did.

Now my problems became trying to figure out what to do with my life, and also I had big issues concerning the opposite sex. Looking back it is easy for me to see that I simply did not know myself at all and had no idea what a healthy relationship would look like.

So there were many bumps in the road.

Rocky times landed me right where I was in 1994 and in the circumstances that I found myself in.

I had eight years clean and sober by this time, but I didn't really have a great job. I didn't really know what I wanted to be when I grew up. And at age twenty-four there had been yet another very painful relationship crash.

Every time I thought I had found "it", perhaps a job, or a woman, the "it" would turn south on me.

My initial Self-Realization came late in the summer.

The realization for me was that, "I am not a musician, I Am Music!"

I had moved to Atlanta (the big city) a year and a half prior to this, and I had been playing music a lot all over the city.

I would work my day job and then off to the gig.

On this particular evening I was filled with sorrow and hurt, depressed, heartbroken, and didn't have anywhere to go, so I decided to sit in my rented room and play guitar for a while.

At some point I stood up, walked across the room and leaned my guitar in the corner. Then I went back and sat down on the bed.

That is when I noticed that the guitar was looking at me.

This was the strangest sensation, but it was indeed looking at me, and so I looked back.

And this is when the light bulb went off in my head.

It all happened fast.

My life flashed before my eyes, and I remembered my very first real guitar lesson at the age of 8. I remembered all the toy guitars I had asked for when my parents would take me to a toy store.

I remembered all the years in my bedroom playing along with records. I remembered all the records I'd had at such an early age.

I had always played music, and had even had a band while in high school.

And here I was playing music 4-5 nights a week around Atlanta and writing my own songs, and ... going to work all day, coming home and actually playing my guitar and thinking, "What am I supposed to do with my life?"

Really?

I was in total shock and disbelief. If it would have been a snake it would have bitten me a thousand times.

How could this be? How could I make a career out of music? How would I survive? Everyone knows you play music on the weekends as a hobby, but it isn't a "real job."

I clearly remember asking God, "Why couldn't I be fascinated with being a doctor or a lawyer or with something that paid well?"

But nevertheless, right then and there I knew my purpose in life and there was absolutely no question.

Music has always seeped out of my pores. I can play anything you put in my hand. I can entertain anyone I wish. Music is my God given natural talent. And at this point, this meant to me that God had put me here to play music.

You are supposed to simply be you. And I knew that.

I got married to God right there. I made the commitment on the spot. It doesn't really matter at that point because things will never be the same, but I did it anyway. I voiced it out loud. "I know now the purpose of my life and this is what I shall do!"

That was in 1994, and today we are in the year 2015, and I have played music ever since and music has been my main income for most of this time. I have a wife, a house, a daughter, a dog, a cat, two turtles and a hamster.

No I am nothing like most people. No I didn't do anything the traditional way.
Looking back I see how I used the exact technique that this book is about most every day.

And now to the reader I want to say that you are holding this book, you are reading these words, for a purpose. We have crossed paths. You are being exposed to this energy.

And it is no mistake.

Nothing is a mistake in the Universe, and this means absolutely nothing.

It is not a mistake that for some reason this book appealed to you, or that someone handed or suggested to you this book.

It wasn't a mistake that before I was eight years old, I was attracted to toy guitars and had a record collection that you wouldn't believe.

It wasn't a mistake that I took my first guitar lesson at such an early age. It wasn't a mistake that music is all I ever really wanted to do.

This obsession, this fascination, this talent and love and dedication that I had for music, was no mistake.

It wasn't difficult either. It was the most natural thing in the world to me.

My parents never had to try and get me to practice. They had to try to get me to stop practicing and come to dinner or do homework, or anything else for that matter.

If there had been a mistake, it would have been that I missed it. We all missed it.

We all thought the same thing; "Music is nice, but how are you going to make a living?"

You are not a mistake. You aren't drawn to the things that you are drawn to by mistake either.

Our passion, the things that we are drawn to, our talents, these are all God trying as hard as It can to tell us which way to go.

God is shining the flashlight for you.

If we are made or created by God, then God made us the way we are. So how could God make us, give us talents and desires, and then make it so that we cannot express these in real life manifestation?

That doesn't make sense.

The truth is that when you discover your true self, (which may not be what you are doing, but it is what you really want to do) you cannot fail.

The only thing of importance in my life after that night in 1994 was music.

Everything in my life, everyone in my life, had to now be there to propel my intention.

Everything else had to go.

I affirmed the importance of my realization and stated that if necessary, I would live in the Salvation Army while playing music.

It never has come to that, but I would still hold that very same conviction.

I began to get the local weekly paper. You could see all the venues in town that had live music and you could see who was playing there. Some of these people I knew, and so I could ask them about who to speak with and the process of getting hired.

I also made lots of cold calls.

Once I landed that first gig, then all the others came more easily.

There is no, "What am I going to do if this doesn't work?" You were made by God, and made in a certain way for a certain purpose. When you know what that purpose is, you also know that God would not create you and give you purpose, and then provide no way for this to be fulfilled.

"There is no "Plan B."

This was my motto and perhaps it still is. More than once it came up against opposition, but nevertheless, I held tightly to it.

Lots of times over the years I forgot and thought that I had to push, to hold on, to "climb the ladder" so to speak.

I forgot that God naturally made me the way I was and that the way I was could just unfold naturally in the world.

My forgetting made things a lot different than they could have been.

But then I would remember again. I would let go again. I would stop pushing and scratching again.

The entire idea of this book is for me to share myself with you, because you and I are One.

All this that I've found is also true for you.

You long for something but you don't know what it is.

Or maybe you know what you want to do but it seems impossible and impractical.

You have a thousand excuses as to why you cannot do it.

It is my job to let you know or at least say to you that you are a Creation of the Creator. You were created for a reason and with a purpose.

When you discover this reason and purpose, know there has also been a way prepared for this to manifest into reality.

Creation does not make the idea without the ability to manifest. You would not be able to think about it if it wasn't possible.

This is the major key to using the technique in this book. This is about knowing that you know.

And you do know.

Solving the Puzzles of Life

Chapter One
The Technique

"Truth is not something outside to be discovered, it is something inside to be realized."
OSHO

It is on the tip of your tongue. You ate at a new restaurant just yesterday and now you are telling your friends about it. But what is the name? You remember where it is, what it looked like, and that they have really great food there.

Yet somehow the name just won't come to you.

You try really hard to remember seeing the sign that is on the door of the restaurant, or anything that will help you remember, but it is of no use. It isn't going to come to you.

So you say, "I can't remember but it will come to me".

You know that you know. You have heard the name, spoken the name, and even been to the restaurant. And so you forget about it for the time being.

Know that it will come to you.

It may be a moment, or it may even be some time the next day while you are grocery shopping. But it will come, and it will come strong. "That's it!" you'll say.

You have now demonstrated exactly how to work the Puzzle of Life.

This is the exact process that you can use to find out the answers to anything.

This is the technique.

It may be that you have always had an inner desire to own your own business, but have been afraid to take the chance. You might think that you don't really have the same chances or opportunities in life that other people have.

You may have your own business already, and you need to know how to make it grow.

You might be struggling through life with addictions, and no matter how hard you've tried; your addictions are still winning. Many of us know about alcoholism and addiction and many of us have suffered or known someone who has suffered the consequences of addiction.

Many of us have unhealthy habits that we would like to change.

Some people just simply feel unsatisfied, and they don't know why. They feel that they are here on this planet to
do something, to accomplish something, but what it is,
remains a mystery to them.

All the answers that you will ever need are already inside of you!

Just like you command that the name of the restaurant will come, you can command the answer to anything.

And it will come.

Most people that I have shared this example of forgetting the name of a restaurant with will say, "That happens to me all the time!"

They are correct, because it happens to us all. But it happens unknowingly!

The Universe that we live in operates according to certain laws, and these laws are in effect at all times. We are subject to these laws, and thus we are already creating our lives, weather we are doing it consciously, or unconsciously.

We need answers, we need resources, we need ideas, and we need to understand certain things.

The most important thing to understand is that nothing is out of your reach in this Universe.

Everything is available to all of us.
Primarily in this book, we are going to focus on and discuss the law of "Cause and Effect."

This law states simply that every cause has an effect and every effect becomes the cause of something else. This means that the universe is always in motion and progressed from a chain of events.

As we will discover in this book and while using this technique, our puzzles are typically a result of us not knowing the true cause.

We can use the technique to find out the true cause, and then we can even find out how to eliminate the cause, or the "blockage" within us that is creating the puzzle.

The Universe is all around you, it is communicating with you even now in this moment.

You are the Universe.

Puzzle of Life Technique
- You think about it really hard.
- You know that you know.
- You are clear about what you want.
- You say the words, "It will come to me."
- You completely release it, knowing that it will come.

Chapter Two
Knowing That You Know

"It follows that everything that Spirit thinks must take form. The Spirit, being Self-Conscious Life, knows and cannot stop knowing."
Ernest Holmes

Puzzle of Life Technique
- You think about it really hard.
- You know that you know.
- You are clear about what you want.
- You say the words, "It will come to me."
- You completely release it, knowing that it will come.

The technique is very easy when it involves something as in our example from Chapter One. You know that you know the name of the restaurant, because you have said it a hundred times, and you have eaten there, and so you know that you know.

You have experienced knowing the name. This is why it is so easy for you to practice the technique.

When we begin to deal with things that we have not experienced, we will have to be just as sure.

And this is the trick.

If you say, "I know that I know and it will come to me" but then you continuously try and remember, it won't come to you. It will remain out of your reach.

When you want to lose weight, make more money, start your own business, find a love partner, stop an unhealthy habit, or do anything that you have not experienced, how can you expect to "Know that you know?"

After all, if you knew, then you would have absolutely no use for a book such as this, would you?

Why do I do the things I do? Why don't I do the things I want to do? Why do I continue an unhealthy habit, knowing that it hurts me? Why can't I seem to find the "right one?" Why can I not forgive a person?

We don't consciously know. We have not had the experience of being the way we want to be or of doing the things we want to do, or of knowing what we want to know.

The most important element to this technique is that you discover that all the answers in the Universe do in fact, reside within you.

You do not know of your own Power, and so you do not know how to use it correctly.

Jesus told us, "Behold! The Kingdom of Heaven is at hand!" This to me signifies that we are currently in Heaven.
Can you imagine being in "Heaven" yet not having something that you need? Can you imagine being in "Heaven" and not having answers?

In Buddhism we are taught that enlightenment involves the uncovering of what is already there. In other words, we are already enlightened; we just don't know it yet.

You can see and experience the Kingdom of Heaven right where you are right now, and you can uncover and discover the Light that is already within you. The Light that you already are.

I want to convince you that you do know, that you have the answers within you and that you have access to those answers.

If you are not totally convinced, you will pressure yourself very hard to try and remember the name of the restaurant. "What is it?" you will repeatedly ask yourself as you strain your mind to recall.

But we know that it won't come to you while you are pressuring it. Only after you have said, "I know that I know and it will come to me" and then you completely let it go, will it come.

Typically we become obsessed with our problems or our puzzles, if you will. "It" is all we think about. Our lives
become consumed by "it." The relationship, the money,
the unhealthy habit, whatever "it" may be "it" takes a very prominent role in our life.

But this doesn't make the problem or puzzle go away or fix it does it?

It is our inability to "leave it alone" that keeps the Universe from being able to help us or provide us with what we need in order to solve the puzzle.

I often work with people who have been dealing with a particular puzzle for a long period of time. As frustration sets in, we may pray to God, we may ask for help or guidance or strength. People try all sorts of things to overcome their puzzles. But we don't get what we pray for.

We continue to practice the bad habit, we continue to sabotage ourselves, and when things don't change, we sometimes wonder what we did to God to deserve this. We wonder what we might have done to cause this, and we wonder why God won't help us.

But when we turn a puzzle/problem into an infatuation or an obsession, what is happening is that our focus is on the puzzle/problem. And so we keep creating it over and over again day after day and year after year.

This also uses up all of our energy.

Suppose there was a sore on your arm, and it developed a scab. The scab actually is part of the healing process, but what happens if you peel off the scab? It grows back and then you peel it off again? Then you are prolonging the healing process and the sore may never go away!

Suppose you were at work and you asked a secretary to please get you a cup of coffee. Then before she can leave to get your coffee, you ask her, "Hey, did you see that show on television last night?" "Did you get that file from the other department yesterday?" "What do you think about this new bill that is up before Congress right now?"

How is she supposed to go get your coffee if you keep asking her questions or keep on talking to her?

This is what you are doing when you cannot "let it go." When you just keep pushing and pushing to remember the name of the restaurant. When you just keep peeling off the scab, asking question after question, and obsessing over a problem or a puzzle; you aren't giving the Universe a chance to heal your sore, bring you coffee, or provide you with the answers to your puzzle.

If you have had an issue in your life that you have struggled with for a period of time, it is more than likely that you are caught up in the reality of, "We create more of what we focus on."

Our puzzles and issues become an obsession that we hold on to and work with night and day. They become very deeply embedded over time and at a certain point they are always there.

In the past, I have created financial problems for myself, and financial problems have branches that spread out to every little nook and cranny of your life.

"How much is it going to cost?" "How much do we have in the bank?" "How much am I making this week?" "Do we have enough money to pay the electric bill?"

But then it goes deeper because every time I would get in my car I would calculate how much fuel I had, where I needed to drive to, and try to figure out just how long I could go before refueling.

You can then begin to ration your food buying, your clothes buying, and before you know it, that "money problem" is the only thing you are thinking about. It can get so deeply embedded and you can get so used to it that you don't notice anymore.

After all, you are thinking about how far you can drive on this tank of gasoline, not about your money trouble. Right?

This became my reality. It became how I felt. It became what I spoke. And so for the longest time it wouldn't go away. It took a lot of work to change the conditions in my life, but using this technique I was able to finally be successful.

What we are doing under these circumstances is totally against the technique in that we don't know that we know. So we continue to focus on it. We continue to pester it. And we continue to keep it.

The command that I gave over and over again for many years was, "I want more money!"

That was basically what I said repeatedly in a thousand different ways, such as, "It sure would be nice." "I wish we had that." or "If I could (had lots of money) I would do this or that."

My entire being became an existence of "lack." And so this was my world.

The only true way to be able to "let it go and forget about it" is for you to know that you know.

The simple truth is that life isn't supposed to be so difficult. The truth is that you can learn how to instruct the Universe to do what you want it to do, and then direct your focus elsewhere.

The Universe is standing by, waiting for your instructions. Once you have given the command, it is time to leave it alone and let the Universe do its part.

The Puzzle of Life Technique
- You think about it really hard.
- You know that you know.
- You are clear about what you want.
- You say the words, "It will come to me."
- You completely release it, knowing that it will come.

This is because the technique will not work if you don't practice it.

We can develop a working communication with the Universe, and the Universe will tell us anything we ask. But we must be able to trust and have faith. Even more than that, we must know. So that we can truly let it go.

Knowing that you know is the only thing that will allow for answers to come to you.

You are going to come to understand and know your Power. You are going to come to understand that the Universe is not against you. God is not punishing you. Now you are going to learn to use your Power in a way that will produce the results you want.

Chapter two questions:

1. After reading through this book, now it is time for you to make your command. It is time to state what you want, what you want to change, or what you want to know.

    I invite you to write it out on paper, but also say it aloud. Feel good now and "know that you know." Release it.

2. Now I invite you to sit down and make a list of all the things and people that are in your life that you like.

    What I am searching for here is to find out what you like about your life.

    Often our focus is so strongly attached to our puzzle and what we don't like, that it may be difficult to steer your mind away from it.

    But steering the mind away is what we will have to do if we want this technique to work. Knowing that we know, we will make our request/command and then we must leave it alone.

    We must learn to put our focus elsewhere, thus the list of things that we like in our lives.

    Once we have this list, then any time we catch ourselves obsessing over the puzzle, we can re-direct ourselves onto something positive from our list.

3. What are some ways that I can place more focus on the people that I care about? Can I call them? Send a card? What nice things can I do to nurture these relationships?

4. What are some ways that I can focus on things that I like in my life? Have I been taking any free time for enjoyment or hobbies? Can I get involved in a project around the yard or the house?

Get busy and stay busy with your focus on the people and things that you are grateful for.

Chapter Three
How We Communicate With The Universe

"The sixth of the seven Universal Laws tells us that 'Every cause has an effect; every effect has its cause.' In accordance with this Law, every effect you see in your outside or physical world has a very specific cause which has its origin in your inner or mental world."
Tania Kotsos

Every part of our Universe is a vibration. There is nothing in the world that is not a vibration. What makes any certain object what it is, is the frequency that it is vibrating at.

And this holds true for us as individuals. It is true that what we eat becomes us. It is true that what we experience becomes us. It is true that each individual part of our body is a vibration. It is true that even our thoughts are vibrating out to the Universe.

When there is a life condition that appears for me that I don't like, I know that it is appearing because this is a vibration that is somehow coming from me. Even if I don't know how or from where it is coming.

Let's examine all the ways in which we vibrate. Our vibrations are our communication to the Universe, and so we will want to become very familiar with them.

We send signals from the
- subconscious mind (these are your past associations) and the
- conscious mind (these are your feelings, thoughts, and words which are all based on past associations).

The Subconscious Mind
We will imagine that the subconscious mind is a computer hard drive.

The subconscious mind is tremendous in size. It is made up of not only what is on the desktop right now, but also all the programs that are beneath the surface.

What is on my desktop right now isn't even one tenth of one percent of what is my hard drive.

I am not a computer programmer, but I know that there are thousands of things happening behind the scenes, in order for me to create this document that is currently on my desktop.

There are lots of programs and codes on the hard drive, which make up these programs. Some of which we are aware of, but many that we are not aware of.

There are also many programs and applications on this hard drive that I am not using right now. However, I know that with the simple push of a button, they will open for me.

But this subconscious hard drive is a bit different than the one in a computer, because information is constantly being added to the subconscious mind.

Every second of every day, our programs are being expanded, and we are creating new programs.

Scientists tell us that the mind is a recording device and that it records everything. We've all heard that "If you could use all of your brain, you would remember your ride home from the hospital just after you were born".

Perhaps you would remember being born. There have been some who have claimed to remember being in the womb.

Every second of your life has been recorded in your mind; all the sounds, the temperature, all the smells, everything that your senses experience is recorded and kept. Once it has happened, it cannot un-happen.

This exact moment is being recorded.

Every moment that you experience becomes you. We are to a large degree, made up of our experiences.

Every time we have an experience or encounter a new person, we have a reaction or response.

We either like it or we dislike it, or we decide that it doesn't have anything to do with us. Every experience we have in life is either a negative, positive, or neutral experience.

We have associations with each experience, and these are always with us, even though we are unaware and may not notice. Your experiences stay with you even though they are not in the conscious mind. You may forget and be totally unaware that you have these inside of you, but everything that has ever happened to you is on your hard drive as an association.

This is something that we need to be very aware of. Everything that we experience in our lives, and more importantly, the way we experience things, is added to and stored on our hard drive.

They are actual physical brain neurons which vibrate.

We are made up of our experiences and the associations that we have for each experience. Whatever negative or positive or even neutral experiences we have had are always with us. We carry everything that has ever happened to us around with us everywhere we go, and it becomes our "baggage."

Whether we are aware of it or not, all of this is a part of our vibration and the signals we send to the Universe.

Since the subconscious mind, or the hard drive, is so large, then it stands to reason that a vast majority of our signals are signals that we are not even aware of.

You may run into someone that you haven't seen since high school. Immediately you see the person and remember that you don't like them because they stole your best friend's girlfriend.

Though you haven't thought of this person in years, the instant you see him, the negative association arises from the hard drive.

You may smell a perfume on someone and it may remind you of a pleasant association you have from the past.

A song may come on the radio and bring back a memory association from the past.

The moment you see the person, smell the perfume, or hear the song, your hard drive sends up the associations that go along with them, and you will feel exactly the way you felt in the past.

It is amazing really how something as small as hearing a song that you haven't heard in a long time, can take you back in time so strongly. It may remind you of other people, other smells; it can seem as if you are actually there all over again.

You can relive that time. Why? How?

Because it is all still inside of you.

You have a negative, positive or a neutral association with all of your past experiences. You carry all of the associations created throughout your life with you wherever you go. Even when you haven't thought about an association or experience in years, it is still with you.

Our associations are actually real physical neurons that are inside our brain. They are physical parts of us. And just like everything else in the Universe, they vibrate and this vibration is a signal. It is your vibration.

We become aware that we are sending these signals only when we see them manifest in our outer world.

The "issues," "problems," or "puzzles," are actually being physically vibrated from within and then manifesting in our lives.

The Conscious Mind
We can think of the conscious mind as being what is on the desktop right now. Consciousness is what we are experiencing at any given time.

The conscious mind will serve you right now, wherever you may be. It tries to have whatever information it thinks you may need available for you.

Let's say that right now you are at a familiar mall. Your mind tells you that the coffee shop is halfway down on the left, and that a particular department store is down at the opposite end.

You have several items that you are shopping for and know which stores you want to go to. Your mind gives you a map of the mall from memory, because this is where you are right now, this is what is on your desktop. It is the program you have open right now.

So when you are at a mall you've been to before, your mind will remember where all the stores are.

When you are at the grocery store, your mind will remember where the beans are and what aisle the paper towels are on.

When you are at work, or when you are at home having dinner with your family, these programs that you require will pop up onto the desktop accordingly.

Just as when you open the calendar on your computer, then close it and open up a photo program, etc… all of these programs are below the surface where you don't see them until you need to open them. The rest of the time they are out of view.

Our consciousness is constantly being directed by inner associations and memories that are stored in the subconscious mind. In other words, what is on our desktop right now is actually being created and projected from the hard drive.

We begin to easily see the importance of having more positive associations than negative. As we go through our day, we encounter different situations and different people, and our inner associations provide us with our feelings and thus our words appear.

Every wayshower has told us of the importance of our words. We can use them to create what we want, and we can also use them to create more of what we do not want.

Our general disposition seems to be developed by the associations that we have accumulated throughout our lives.

Our words are formed by our associations, or inner convictions, which is how we feel and what we think.

Even though these associations are not in the conscious mind, they are still there. They are still vibrations and signals that we are sending out. They materialize into our consciousness, or our conscious mind.

People often do not know why they feel the way they feel. They do not know why they have the disposition that they have. "I don't know why I see the glass as half-full." "I do not know why I am depressed all the time."

"Words saturated with sincerity, conviction, faith and intuition are like highly explosive vibration bombs, which, when set off, shatter the rocks of difficulties and create the change desired."
Paramahansa Yogananda

I have heard lots of discussion and theories concerning which comes first, the thoughts or the feelings, and yet I wouldn't feel qualified to say for sure.

What I can say for sure is that negative thoughts and feelings are going to produce negative words. And your word is the Law.

If we are prone to speaking negatively, it is because this is how we feel. This is how we think. The first order of business in this case is to begin changing what we speak. At the very least, stop speaking negativity. Close the door on it. You can use the technique in this book to explore and find out why you think and feel negatively. It stands to reason that if you felt good, and if you were having positive thoughts, then you would speak positively.

"Whatever follows 'I Am' is going to come looking for you."
Pastor Joel Osteen

We can use the technique to discover the negative associations that are creating negativity in our lives. We can then use the technique to find out how to change those negatives into positives. We can feel better. We can speak positively. We can instruct anything from the Universe. As we progress in becoming the vibration that we want to become, anything is possible!

Chapter three questions:

1. Looking back on your life, how would you imagine your past associations? Would you think that you would have more negative associations than positive?

2. Have you ever experienced something that took you back in time? You could have smelled a familiar smell, tasted a familiar food, or run across someone from your past. The moment you encounter something or someone from the past, your brain brings up the associations, and suddenly you feel exactly like you did in the past.

3. Write about your general disposition. Do you see yourself as a positive "glass half full" kind of person? Or are you the opposite?

4. Would you say that you look for the good in things and speak positively?

Chapter Four
Universal Access

This is where things will get very interesting.

The idea that any information in the Universe is readily available to us is hard to imagine, much less, believe.

Even after all of the seemingly "impossible" events that I have experienced and witnessed, it is still sometimes hard for me to make this connection which is: "knowing that I know". Or that it is possible for me to know.

Nevertheless we can agree that whatever answers or whatever information that we would like to obtain, is there somewhere. It must be.

If it is here in existence, then there is a way that we can connect to it.

- Consciousness = Desktop = where you are and what you are doing right now.
- Subconscious = Hard Drive = All previous life experiences.
- Universal Consciousness = the Internet.

The Universal Consciousness
We have discovered that everything in existence is on your own personal hard drive, because your hard drive is connected to everyone else's! This is what is called the "Universal Consciousness".

It appears that your hard drive and mine are connected to this "motherboard" of information that is made up of everyone's hard drive.

I went to Wiki to get a definition and explanation;
Universal Mind may be defined as the nonlocal and atemporal hive mind of all aggregates, components, knowledge's, constituents, relationships, personalities, entities, technologies, processes and cycles of the Universe. The nature of the Universal mind is omniscient, omnipotent, omnificent and omnipresent. It's also the human nature. It's believed that one has access to all knowledge, known and unknown. Through the Universal Mind, people have access to an infinite power; one then is able to tap into the limitless creativity of the One. All these attributes are present within one at all times in their potential form.

The notion of Universal Mind came into the Western Canon through the Pre-Socratic

philosopher Anaxagoras, who arrived in Athens sometime after 480 BC. He taught that all things were created by Nous (Mind) and that Mind held the cosmos together and gave human beings a connection to the cosmos, or a pathway to the divine.
http://en.wikipedia.org/wiki/Universal_mind

Continuing with the computer idea, my daughter came up to me one day with an iPad and said, "Dada type in "Little girls get puppies for Christmas."

So I did.

To my surprise, there were a lot of videos on YouTube of exactly that; little girls getting puppies for Christmas.

The internet is pretty handy! Recently I typed in "how to replace the insides of a toilet" and a very helpful video popped right up. I watched it, and then went and did the job, knowing what to expect and what to do.

I also used this same technique in fixing our oven last year.

You can type in anything at all into a search engine, and get your answer. The Universal Conscious is just like the internet.

All you have to do is know how to ask.

Using the Universal Consciousness, anything that you want to know how to do, anything you want to create, any answer that you want, it is possible for you to access it.

They tell us that it is possible for someone who has never played a piano, to just sit down and start playing.

In his famous book, "Autobiography of a Yogi", Paramahansa Yogananda tells us the story of how he spent so much time with his guru, that he didn't study for his school exams. But when he went to take the exam, he was able to just know all the answers.

Examples of people tapping into the Universal Consciousness are popping up in front of me all the time now. I have been practicing this myself, and I believe all this. I know things like this can happen.

The more I thought about it, the more I realized that to a certain extent I had been doing this for years!

All my life, seemingly unexplainable things have happened to me and I've seen them happen to others.

Once as a teenager I was in my room attempting to learn a particular guitar solo.

Over and over I would attempt to play along with the record, but it was to no avail. There was something that just didn't make sense to me.

At some point I leaned my guitar in the corner and went to bed, only to begin to dream. In the dream, there I was, playing the guitar solo!

"But wait a minute!" I thought. "This is a dream!" The dream was so realistic that in the dream I decided to play the guitar solo a few times until I knew it well. When I woke up from the dream, I got my guitar, and played the guitar solo.

Of course! I'd just done it ten times in the dream and had gotten it "under my thumb". So now I knew.

Somewhere in my subconscious mind or on my hard drive, was the information and knowledge of how to play that guitar solo, and somehow I accessed it. Cases such as this are often referred to as "supernatural."

"Supernatural" from Webster's dictionary:
1. of or relating to an order of existence beyond the visible observable universe; especially: of or relating to God or a god, demigod, spirit, or devil
2.
a: departing from what is usual or normal especially so as to appear to transcend the laws of nature
b: attributed to an invisible agent (as a ghost or spirit)

Of course as a musician, a songwriter, and an artist, I am very familiar with the supernatural. I will be playing guitar, and suddenly there is something that was never there before! A new pattern or note, a new song appears seemingly out of nowhere.

I can just get lost in it. I say, "lost" in it but this may not be correct phrasing, because you are anything but lost, you are totally found. You are connected and there is a vibration, and everyone present knows that you are "on."

When surfers get that look in their eye and talk of "Riding the wave", I think I understand what they mean.

People who follow bands like the Grateful Dead and collect recordings of all their shows have their favorite particular shows. You will hear them say, "They were ON that night!"

If they did twenty-five shows on a particular tour, there was this one show that a majority of the fans conclude was the "best."

But don't be caught in the illusion that only musicians and artists and writers experience this kind of thing. I believe that anyone who is passionate about what they are doing is subject to get into a "flow."

You could be a surgeon or a nurse or an ironworker or an investor or a carpenter, or anything really. You hone your skills, you are doing what you do and sometimes you can stand back and say, "Look at that! Look how awesome that is!"

You know when you are "on."

When dancers get into the flow it is as if they are floating on air. They are so graceful and their movements seem so effortless.

Sometimes athletes in a very competitive game will somehow exceed their normal abilities.

Surgeons, dancers, and athletes are very practiced in their skills. Their lives are dedicated to their craft. They practice and train for years and then they "get out on the field and do it."

And then there are stories like the grandmother who reached down and picked up a car that had rolled onto her grandchild. People sometimes experience superhuman strength, usually in life or death situations.

We know that it is possible to get on these "waves" or "channels" in the mind and ride. We know that we know things that we may not be conscious of. We know that we can possess supernatural and superhuman strength and courage that is beyond what we normally experience.

All the information, all the talent and strength and courage, all the answers, all the songs, all of everything is in there, in the hard drive or the Universal Consciousness.

Thus, we all have access to the tools that we need to do anything we want to do!

You can use the technique in this book to help you access anything that you want to know.

Ask properly, and it will come to you.

The Puzzle of Life Technique
- You think about it really hard.
- You know that you know.
- You are clear about what you want.
- You say the words, "It will come to me."
- You completely release it, knowing that it will come

Chapter four questions:

1. How do you truly feel about the idea of Universal Consciousness?

2. Have you ever tapped into the Universal Consciousness, or known anyone who did?

Chapter Five
Your New Life

"If we did all the things we are really capable of doing, we would literally astound ourselves."
Thomas Edison

Human beings are truly amazing.

We have evolved from living in the most primal fashion, step by step, advancing to where we are today; each moment leading us to the next.

The industrial age and machinery led to the automobile, airplanes, electricity, and now in the modern era of technology, it is no big deal to teleconference in real time with someone who is on the other side of the world.

We strive, we push, and we admire great athletes, great scientists, and great artists. We want to be like them. We want our children to be like them.

Humans are creators. We all feel the urge and the pull, to be more or to do more.

We have ideas. We want to do things, go places, and to feel as if we are living our lives to the fullest.

While some people seem to succeed, there are many who meet opposition and just stop. There is something in the way. There is something that is holding them back. There is some reason why they cannot do what they want.

We look at those we admire, and say things like, "I could never do that" or "I wish I was more like him or her."

We aren't tall enough or short enough. We aren't smart enough or courageous enough. We are overweight and it has always been this way. We can't stop smoking or drinking and start exercising. We don't have enough money. We aren't very good with relationships.

And though we may never say it out loud, there is the idea that those people we see on television or in magazines are better than us. We think they are prettier, smarter, luckier, faster, stronger, and more talented than us.

We think we cannot do it.

But are they really that different? Is there really such a vast ocean of difference between us?

Think what you will, say what you will but everyone wants to succeed with whatever they attempt to do. There are people that we see succeeding and have found success, they have that "something" that we think we don't have.

We think, they know something we don't know, or they have access to something we haven't found access to as of yet.

There are also people who are actively doing and trying to figure it out.
People who are giving it their best shot and when it fails, it can be difficult to try again. This is one of our most challenging aspects of trying to do something. Getting back up and trying to make what we want to succeed or to attempt something else.

"If at first you don't succeed, try, try, try again!"

And then there those who never attempt anything, or they do attempt something, only to never attempt anything again after a failure.

In a way, the failure is much easier.

The world is full of people who cannot even get up the juice to try. They cannot get past their personal problems, the addictions, fear, laziness, or even the knowing what they would do if they could do something.
If they don't put out the big effort or even try, there is no big failure. There are no great disappointments.

There is only the familiar. Life can seem much easier and much safer this way.

Many of us stay there.

People that are stuck in this place find their minds comprised of simple thoughts, ideas, and beliefs. Those thoughts that other people are smarter than they are or others have more drive than they do; others have more ambition, are better looking, or get all the breaks. That these other people simply have what we don't have.

We have a thousand excuses, reasons, justifications, and ways in which we are different than people that try and succeed, or ways in which they are different from us.

People that never try to accomplish anything may even feel a strong dislike for those that succeed.

We think they are "better than" and we are "less than". But perhaps we resent this. Perhaps deep down, we would like to be a success.

But we aren't.

This is the Great Divide, and we are the Creator of it.

It is our own thoughts, ideas, and beliefs that create the chasm between people that succeed and people that fail.

And none of it is true.

Chapter five questions:

1. Are you a person who has never tried? Why?

2. Are you a person who has tried and failed? Write about yourself and how you see yourself. Why do you think you failed? Are you ready to try again? Or to make a go at something else?

3. Everyone has something or a few things that they would love to do, but are convinced that these things would be impossible. Things like scuba-diving, travel to exotic locations, parachuting out of an airplane, or starting your own business. Whatever the desire may be, we have reasons why we cannot actually do what we would like to do.

    Write about your "impossible dream or dreams."

4. How can you use our technique, to help you accomplish your "impossible dream?" What are some commands you could give? What do you need to know?

5. I am going to invite you now to choose an "impossible dream," and use the technique in this book to help you achieve it. Get a journal or notebook specifically for this adventure. And send me pictures of yourself living your "impossible dream!"

Chapter Six
It's Nothing Personal

> "What the mind of man can conceive and believe, it can achieve."
> **Napoleon Hill**

The Universe operates on a system of Laws. There is the "Law of Cause and Effect", the "Law of Mind Action", and the "Law of Attraction." These Laws are not negotiable. They don't waver.

Just like with the Law of Gravity, if you throw a ball up into the air, it is coming back down. This is not personal in any way. This is just the way that things operate.

Notice how when we think we are failures, our thoughts, ideas, and beliefs, are all of the personal nature? We have decided that other people are better than us. We have decided that other people have things and qualities that we don't have.

We are using the Universal Laws already. The Universe is giving us what we think and believe. It is giving us what we tell it to give us.

Successful people tell us that, "Anybody can do this!" To them it is a simple matter of the Law of Cause and Effect. "You do this, and you get that." There is nothing personal about this!

A person can just as easily begin giving different instructions and signals to the Universe.

Napoleon Hill did not say, "The mind of the LUCKY man" or "The mind of just a few men." He said, "The mind of MAN."

The Law of Cause and Effect or the Law of Attraction will work exactly the same way for you, as it will for anyone else. The Laws are not personal.

The difference between someone who is a success and someone that feels they are a failure is their thoughts, ideas, and beliefs.

These can be changed.

The great inventor Thomas Edison never questioned for a second the possibility of a light bulb. He knew that it was a possibility, and though it took him more than twenty years of experimenting, he finally figured it out.

It wasn't a question of, "Can I invent a light bulb?" it was a matter of gathering the correct elements. Mr. Edison had every element known to man in his laboratory, and he experimented with many of them in many different ways, before he finally figured it out. But he figured it out.

Over twenty years! Can you imagine that? Failure after failure, one experiment after another gone awry, we can easily imagine that nobody in history has ever failed more times than Edison.

But it was never of a personal nature to him. He never saw it as a personal thing, or thought that he wasn't good enough or smart enough. It was totally impersonal.

It was a matter of fact; it was a matter of Law.

He knew that if he could imagine it in his mind, that there was a way to do it. He knew that there was nothing personal about inventing this light bulb. He knew that whoever put the correct elements together in the correct way, would have a light bulb.

It is the same as adding two plus two and getting four. This is completely impersonal. Any one of us can do it!

Mr. Edison knew it wasn't personal, and he became determined to find the way, and that is the only difference between a man like him who succeeds and a man who fails, or who does not try at all.

Now is the time to realize that yes, we are all different in our own ways. Each person is unique and special in his or her own way.

It must be pointed out at this point that this technique is not to get you to be like someone else. That isn't the point here. The idea is to be YOU.

The idea is that you are supposed to be you. You are supposed to want the things you want. You are supposed to evolve and grow and face challenges and overcome them. These are all the reasons for life!

We can overcome any challenge that we may face, and it is nothing personal.

I know that you have talents and good qualities about you that would serve yourself and others. I know you can make a difference in the world in a positive way.

I know that there is somewhere in the world that you haven't been, that you would really like to go. I know there is something you would really like to do that you haven't done. I know that you think you can do better in life, and though I love you just like you are, I know that you can do what you want to do.

That is why we are here!

Creator's create. We are supposed to evolve. We are supposed to get better and go further. We are supposed to push the limits. We are supposed to evolve even further still.

How could this be if we didn't have the necessary tools? How could this be if we weren't in fact built this way?

You are supposed to be you. You are supposed to like what you like. You are supposed to want what you want. You are supposed to better yourself and grow.

This is what life is all about.

The intention of this book is to tell you that you have all the tools, tell you what they are, and finally, to help you learn to use them.

Are you willing to let go of the thoughts, ideas, and beliefs that fill the space between you and people of category one? Can you move past the personal nature and into the impersonal nature of the Universal Laws? "If he or she can do it, then I can do it too!"

Chapter six questions:

1. With the things you want to change about yourself, or with the things you would like to do, can you see how you have made it all personal?

2. How have you been out of line with Universal Laws?

3. Write out and make a case for what you want, and show how it is not personal. What Universal Laws can you use, and how can you bring yourself more in line with the Laws?

Chapter Seven
Anything Really Is Possible!

"Each person comes into this world with a specific destiny – he has something to fulfill, some message has to be delivered, some work has to be completed. You are not here accidentally – you are here meaningfully. There is a purpose behind you. The whole intends to do something through you."
OSHO

When it comes to desiring change in our lives, we either want to change something that is inside of us, or we want to change our external reality. So let's separate these into two groups or patterns:

Our Patterns and Signals
- Negative Life Patterns = Self sabotage and bad habits
- Unfulfilled dream patterns = unfulfilled wishes

Negative Life Patterns
When we are stuck in a negative life pattern, it is because we don't know how to get out of it. We sometimes think we know what is causing it, but not always.
Even when we know or have a good idea of the cause, we don't know what to do about that. So the pattern continues.

But we all know the truth that nobody does this to us. We do these things to ourselves. Examples of this are alcoholism, addiction, overeating, nail biting, depression, being late, or any form of self-sabotage.

With these negative life patterns, we hurt our chances in life, we hurt our friends and family and people who care about us, but most of all, ourselves.

We battle these negative life patterns or habits, but yet they persist.
- Because we don't know the true cause of the pattern, or
- We do know the true cause, but we don't know how to clear it.

Often times, people can only surrender and endure their negative life patterns. "Oh well, this is just the way I am." or "Oh well, I've always been this way."

These negative statements and ideas only serve to perpetuate the problem.

And so we go through life the best we can, but all the while we are suffering.

Meanwhile, there is a cause to your negative life pattern, and there is also a way to clear or heal the cause.

The cause and the cure both exist.

Change is possible!

Just because I have been this way all my life doesn't mean that I can't change.

When we discover the cause and the cure of our negative life patterns, they will begin to slip away, in a seemingly effortless fashion.

Unfulfilled Dream Patterns
When there is something that we want to do and we don't do it, this is because we do not see a way. It does not seem possible to us because we simply don't see the path.

When we cannot see a path, it appears to us to be impossible. We want more money, the new car, a new house, or to start a new business; maybe we have always wanted to scuba-dive or learn to play an instrument, these all fall under this group or pattern.

All we see are the barriers and the reasons why we cannot do these things or have these things.

Imagine there are five thousand acres of woods, and we know that there is a campsite somewhere in there, but there is no path. There are trees and bushes and thorns and many dangerous things, but no path leading us to where we want to go.

But our reasoning will tell us that if there is a campsite in there, then there must be a way to get to it. Otherwise, how would anyone have built the campsite to begin with? There must be a path.

We just don't know where it is. We just don't see it.

So we are left standing there seeing only the barriers and making no movement towards our dream.

We just keep on dreaming.

But we have agreed that if there is a campsite, there has to be a way to get to it. In this same way, if there is a dream, there has to be a way to fulfill it!

The money, the car, the new house, the business you want to start, the ocean you want to scuba-dive in, and the instrument you want to play already are there in existence.

It would be impossible for there not to be a path.

Chapter Eight
An Orderly Process

> *"The law of divine creation is perfect order and harmony."*
> **Charles Fillmore**

We want to grow and change, and we know that this is entirely possible, but we don't know how.

This great Universe of ours works in a very orderly fashion. The one thing that you need to know as you begin this practice is that in order to go from A to Z, you must involve all the other letters.

You can develop a working open communication line between yourself and God/the Universe, but you will often find that there are no shortcuts.

In some cases people will experience big sudden positive changes, but rest assured that these changes will not happen unless you are on that plane.

Unless you are prepared, it cannot happen. Unless it is for your Highest Good, the Universe will intercede.

Sometimes people get that job they have been wanting, or find the love of their life. Other times someone may suddenly get fired from a job, or their spouse may leave them.

You want to change your life. You are learning to communicate and have a working relationship with the Universe.

The guarantee that comes with this technique is that things are going to change.

If things quickly change for the better, then that is wonderful, but if "bad" things suddenly happen, know that this is just the Universe clearing the way for you.

Often the first things that people want to ask for are things like, "I want to lose sixty pounds." "I want that $60,000 Mercedes." Or "I want to be rich and successful!"

Typically you will get no results from these commands, because you are wishing to move in an unorderly fashion.

What you will want to do at this point, is lay out a well-designed plan, that sees you beginning at point A and ending at point Z.

Your plan may very well seem outlandish to you, but let's remember the people who made a plan to fly. How about the people who flew to the moon; or the people who invented electricity and the internet? Certainly those ideas were more far-fetched than any I've ever had. Far-fetched? They were downright impossible.

Or were they?

Whatever idea that you have is not impossible! What is impossible is to have an idea that is impossible!

> *"The journey of a thousand miles begins with one single step."*
> ***Lao Tzu***

Make a plan and begin today. The sooner you begin on your journey, the sooner you will feel better. The moment you take the first step is an indication that you have changed.

Now this has become "something you are in the process of doing", rather than something you wish you could do. Now you are a "doer" rather than a "wisher." You will fulfill that dream.

What we have in our favor is that we all have some experience with this.

Everyone on some level has made a plan and followed through with it. A plan can be as simple as standing up, walking across the house to the bathroom, and relieving yourself, or as big as going through school and getting a Masters or a P.H.D. Every success that you may see began with "the first step."

Are you ready to take that "first step"?

Chapter eight questions:

1. In past endeavors, have you had extreme thinking? Have you tried to go from A to Z without all the steps in between?

2. Writing out your current goals and intentions, draw a map that includes all the steps necessary to achieve your goal. Create a pathway from where you are to where you want to go.

3. Now take that first step!

Chapter Nine
Change the Question

"The majority of men meet with failure because of their lack of persistence in creating new plans to take the place of those which fail."
Napoleon Hill

If we closely examine this technique and ourselves, we will see that our entire reality is shaped by vibrations that we have been unaware of. These are our past experiences and associations that we carry around with us inside.

Therefore, it is not uncommon for someone to have no idea what is causing an unpleasantness. It is there, it won't seem to go away, but we really don't know why.

We cannot relate to it.

We now know that it is coming from within. However, we don't relate to it because we may not have even thought about this association for decades. But we know that if it is appearing in our outer reality, it is a part of our inner reality.

Somewhere on the hard drive lies the culprit.

You may have an intention and a plan drawn out. Yet as you begin to take the necessary steps toward the changes you want to make, things don't work out.

As an example, when working with someone who has a food and weight problem, the initial command may be, "I want to be skinny!"

Weight problems are very common in our world and many times the first idea that someone will have is, "I'll go on a diet!" Diet books are, and have been for quite some time, the best-selling books.

Often they don't work so well.

When they do seem to work and someone loses weight, it is only a matter of a short time before the old habits come back along with the weight. Along with the weight come the frustrations, the self-loathing, and all of the negativity that we are familiar with.

We have given the command, "I want to lose weight" a million times now and it isn't working. The person may have tried many diets by now, and they aren't working either. So what to do now?

What if we were to change the command?

Change the question
Instead of commanding, "Make me skinny" or "Make me rich" or "Make my business or relationship successful," now is the time to use the technique to find out, "What is blocking me from my good?"

We can tell the Universe to show us what is within us that is keeping us from what we want.

We at this point obviously know that we have negative associations somewhere within that are serving to hold us back. Where are they? What are they?

In other words, I command the Universe to bring it into my awareness.

Once we can identify these associations that are blocking us, we can then proceed in changing them.

It is a fact that when we instruct the Universe accordingly, it will bring it to us on a silver platter.

Now, instead of the signal we have been giving or continuing to ask for something specific we are going to ask:
- "What is blocking me?"
- "How am I blocking myself?"
- "What is my resistance to this?"

The signal I like to use is "Show me what is blocking me from _____"
Often I will add, "And when you show me, please make it obvious so that I cannot miss it!"

Now we have shifted our command from, "I want to lose weight" to "Show me what is blocking me from losing weight."

What we are doing is developing a communication between us and our deepest inner self.

What you will find
When we decide to shift our command from "Give me that" or "Create this in my life", to "Show me what is blocking me from what I want", we must be prepared for something out of the ordinary to happen.

After all, we are doing something different and out of the ordinary by now. We are taking responsibility that the situation is indeed coming from within us, and we have changed our command in regards to the situation.

Sometimes it is uncomfortable because, remember, it is a hidden negative association that will appear. This not always the case, there are also times when a positive association will appear.

The Universe is going to give us what we need when we need it.

I have had people that I haven't seen since childhood, suddenly appear into my life.

I have gone in to work where as far as I knew, everything was okay, only to be fired.

I have also had people that I didn't know walk up to me and give me exactly what I needed at the time.

These things happen seemingly out of the blue, but when we've given the command, the Universe has to respond.

We haven't known the true cause of our problem, and so we are most often surprised when it arrives.

In the mind there is usually one or two ways that we can see a situation working out. In the larger scheme of things though, you will find that the Universe has a bigger bag of tricks than we can know.

This always reminds me of the Rubik's Cube puzzle. Remember, there are over forty-three quintillion different solutions to the Rubik's Cube. It is one little cube or puzzle that you can hold in your hand, and yet there are more ways to solve it than the mind can image.

That is exactly how our "problems" are. There are more ways to solve them than our minds can comprehend.

The Puzzle of Life Technique
- You think about it really hard.
- You know that you know.
- You are clear about what you want.
- You say the words, "It will come to me."
- You completely release it, knowing that it will come

Know that you know! Now you give the command and then drop it and forget about it.

And you will soon see that your deepest inner self will always answer, and is always answering you.

Rest assured, if you are listening and watching, the Universe will make it clear to you what is blocking you. When we want to change something, we must find out what the cause is. This is where the work must be done.

You will soon see exactly how you are giving conflicting signals.

Are we making conflicting statements? Are we having conflicting thoughts? Is there something from our past that is haunting us via the subconscious mind?

If our outer world is not to our liking, it can only be because we are sending mixed messages to the Universe and it can only respond accordingly. We are not being clear. We are not in alignment.

In other words, what we are experiencing in life is our own self.

Thus, if we give a command and don't see results, this indicates that even though we may be commanding more money, or a healthy relationship, or whatever it may be, there is something inside of us that is afraid or doesn't think we deserve it, or that we are not good enough for it.

Are you sending mixed messages?

At one point in my life, there was a particular kind of car that I wanted. I envisioned myself driving it, thought about it often, and began to notice them all over the place.

One day while sitting at a red light, I saw a man getting out of a very pretty car, made by the same company as the car I wanted. "Hmph" I said. "He could have done a lot of good works with that money."

WHAT??? Here I was trying to manifest myself into having a very expensive automobile, but when I saw someone who had a very expensive automobile, I dismissed them as being selfish.

The Universe showed me my inconsistency. On one hand I want it, but on the other hand, I am saying that I don't. That is pretty confusing for the Universe because I am simply confused.

I realized that I would have felt self-conscious and guilty if I had this car. The more I explored my inner feelings, the more I saw that I had drawn lines between myself and "my kind", and "them."

"Them" being people with money and wealth. Somehow I saw them as being on the "other team." I also realized that I thought they were better and smarter than me. It was a "what side of the tracks are you from" kind of thing.

This stuff was rooted so deeply in me that I couldn't believe it. I could instantly become defensive, self-righteous, and at the very same time, envious.

This is unharmonious. This is sending two vibrations that don't harmonize. Just as if you play two music notes that are not harmonizing, you get an unpleasant sound. When we send vibrations that are not in harmony, we get an unpleasant circumstance.

When you start working with this technique, the Universe is going to point out your inconsistent messages. You are going to suddenly find yourself somewhere that hurts, or around someone that is painful to be around. Negative associations that we carry within us create negative circumstances in our lives. Now that the Universe has shown you and you are aware, the only thing you can do is to own up to it and admit it.

But then you have to work it out and make sense of it inside.

In every case we are saying that we want a particular thing or circumstance, but at the same time we are saying that we don't. We have to explore this and how we truly feel. We have to come to a conclusion about it that is straight and true.

And this is how we change our past associations.

The Universe will show you what it is that is blocking you.

The simple fact is that if the Universe isn't giving you what you want, it is because of you. You are giving the command, but there is something in your inner self that is giving an opposite command.

This is commonly the stuff that is easier to avoid. We have very deep-seated beliefs that we aren't worthy, or that we aren't smart, or that we aren't "good enough". Someone told us, or we told ourselves that we would never be successful, and deep down we believe that.

Someone may command a healthy relationship, and in the next breath say, "I'm not very good when it comes to the opposite sex."

Someone may ask for more money while at the same time believing that, "Money is the root of all evil."

The Universe can only show us what we are. The Universe can only give us what we instruct it to give us. Our outer lives are truly a reflection of our inner lives. If on the inside we have negative beliefs about ourselves, it will do no good to command more money.

How it happens sometimes
Not in every case, but quite often when we look back on our lives, we see that a situation we thought was terrible, worked out for the best in the long run.

The relationship that went sour, the great job we lost, the thing that didn't go our way, simply opened the door to new and better things in our life. We also sometimes see that we have gotten what we wanted, only to find that it wasn't anything like we thought it would be.

Perhaps we enrolled in a field of study only to find that we were not at all interested in it. Our "dream date" turned out to be a "bad dream." Maybe we worked and pushed our way into a job position, and then thought, "Why did I do this to myself?"

This indicates that we don't always know what is "good" or "bad" for us. The lesson we can learn from this awareness is that when something shifts in our life, we don't have to immediately overreact. It doesn't have to be so exciting, nor does it have to be so upsetting.

It may be sudden and take us by surprise, but we can remember that whether it appears to us "good" or "bad," we can't be too sure.

There was the man who had worked his way up the ladder at work and now he was in a management position. Not only was he a manager, his department was doing really well.

This man had been very adamant that he "just wanted to find his place in life."

This job had fallen into his lap, he had excelled at it, and so he figured, "This is it, I am a salesman!"

One day he came into work and was told that he was being fired for "improper handling of money."

Then he was told that there had been an investigation and that the company knew that he had done nothing wrong, "But word got out about the investigation and it looks bad and so we have to let you go." He was told.

All of his plans and dreams came crashing down around him and he was devastated. He put his belongings into his car and moved away to another city.

Soon he would find his true calling of being a musician. And then he understood.

He had thought so much of his old job, and thought that his life then was great; but now he saw that it was nothing compared to his new life. A life which never would have come without the rearranging.

This man also shared with me that in his music career he uses things he learned from that sales job almost every day. He feels now that the Universe had put him in the sales position, so that he could learn what he needed to know for his next journey.

Never had he imagined playing music for a living, even though music was and always had been, his true love.

He had been commanding to the Universe, "Tell me what I am." And "Tell me what you want me to do."

And the Universe told me. (Yes, this happened to me.)

There was another man who had been attending a certain church and had been feeling the calling to go into ministry.

He attended some classes, and then went to a weekend convention put on by the organization, and after the Saturday night program, he became totally convinced that he wanted to become a minister.

"It was the most magical night of my life." He told me. "I was walking along the river with friends, and there were fireworks across the river, and it was just so exhilarating to be there and to finally know what I wanted to do with my life."

Upon returning to his room, he called home, and his wife told him that she was leaving and that she wanted a divorce.

At the time he had been devastated. How could something so terrible happen just when something so wonderful had happened?

This man is a minister now, and a close friend of mine. It has been over ten years since his experience that night, and here is what he has to say about it now: "I am so glad that she isn't in my life anymore, and I don't know what I was thinking to begin with."

When you start really talking to the Universe, the Universe is going to talk back. Understand that if something is suddenly taken away or something suddenly changes, that this is a necessary event that is bringing you closer to what you want.

Ideally we will learn to trust in the Universe and to know that it is not against us. In reality it cannot be against us. No person can work against us either, because the Universal Laws are much stronger than any individual person.

We get the feeling that wherever we are and whatever the conditions are, is right where we are supposed to be.

Chapter nine questions:

1. If there is a puzzle that you have had for a long time, we know that you have been giving the wrong command, or asking the wrong question. Thus we have to change the command or the question. Now we can ask questions like, "What is blocking me from this?" or "What is truly causing this?"

2. Often what the Universe shows us is going to be painful. We must remember that the cause is negative associations in the brain. Once you make the command, the Universe will bring it to you and show you. Are you prepared to deal with painful situations from your past?

3. Are there situations that come to mind that you are not prepared to deal with?

4. Remember that you can also use this technique to command, "Show me how to heal from this." Once again, the Universe has no choice but to show you. Whatever the case, the negative associations can be turned into positive.

5. Look for mixed messages. Do you say one thing one minute, but then rebuke it in some way the next? Are you saying that you want something, but then not making any changes in your life or moves towards what you say you want? Write about how you can be more harmonious and stop sending mixed messages.

Chapter Ten
Changing the Associations

"Yesterday I was clever, so I wanted to change the world. Today I am wise, so I am changing myself."
Rumi

The Universe has now brought into your life and made clear to us our negative associations that are blocking us from our good. This is when we get to truly face that we have been sending inconsistent signals to the Universe.

What a beginning we have made! Now we know the associations or where the negative vibrations are coming from, so we can change them.
- Awareness and being conscious
- Changing our words
- Affirmations
- Re-framing

Awareness and being conscious
How amazing it is that we now have a way to increase our awareness. After all, this is what our experience here is all about. Becoming "enlightened" or "awakened" depends on our increasing awareness.

As long as we are seeking and we have a spiritual practice, we can rest assured that we are moving in a direction of growth.

Knowing what we now know about the hard drive and how it is constantly recording and then vibrating the contents, we will now be more conscious about what we allow to go in there. This means that we will become more selective about who we spend time with, where we go, what we do, what we watch on television or the music we listen to. Every single little detail is being recorded and becoming your inner self, so every single little detail matters greatly.

Just as physical pain lets us know when something is out of line with the body, emotional pain lets us know when something is out of line in the mind.

It is the situations which cause us pain and discomfort that we want to change. There will be times when what used to be quite comfortable will become just as uncomfortable. This is simply because of our evolution.

All things in the Universe are evolving and moving, and that includes us. Therefore you will find at times that what used to work doesn't anymore. We can rest in the knowing that our pain is simply a signal that it is time to evolve. We can rest in the knowing that we are supposed to evolve, and that we will evolve. We can rest in the knowing that we can evolve.

All that we have to do is command the Universe, and we will be given what we have asked for. We will be given the answers we have asked for.

And we will see.

Once I attended a meditation program that was presented by a traveling man named Swami Ken. It was held at a local Yoga Center and on their website there was information about Swami and what the program would entail.

There would be short introduction followed by a one hour meditation and then Swami would give a short talk. It also stated that Swami Ken would transmit a blessing to each of us, via his guru Sri Shivabalayogi Maharaj, who had "dropped his physical form" in 1994.

You cannot imagine how intriguing this was to me. Though I began meditating in the mid 80's, here I was all these years later having never gone to a meditation program. I'd definitely never meditated with a yogi before, and the idea of the transmitted blessing from his deceased guru sealed the deal.

I put on some sweat pants and a t-shirt and arrived early for the program.

The room was very crowded and I was very excited to meditate and receive a blessing, when Swami spoke and told us that "The most important thing that is going to happen to you today has already happened. It happened when you decided to come here."

> *"The most important thing that is going to happen to you today has already happened. It happened with you decided to come here for meditation."*
> **Swami Ken**

This was perplexing to me, as someone who was expecting a pretty big experience that day, to find that the most important thing had already happened. I felt a little cheated actually, though the meditation experience was quite nice.

But what Swami said really stuck with me. Since then those words have unfolded in my life and they continue to unfold to this day. What they have come to mean is that "I matter." "It matters." What we spend our time doing, who we spend our time with, it all matters a great deal.

I never really thought I mattered very much before. Therefore, none of the other things really mattered all that much. But now that we have begun on the spiritual path, we will realize just how much we matter and just how much everything matters.

You matter a great deal. As we are promised by Jesus; "Seek and ye shall find."

Changing Our Words
Someone invited me to lunch with a group of friends once and I heard myself say, "I wish I could but I can't because I've got to go pick up my kid."

Now that in general terms is really not that big a deal until you start actually listening to what you are saying.

Then it sounds pretty depressing.

This particular day I caught myself and said, "Wait no, let me rephrase that!"

The second time around it came out like this; "It would be enjoyable to go to lunch with you all, but today I get to pick up my princess and take her to the park to play. We are going on big adventures!"

    A. "I wish I could but I can't because I've got to go pick up my kid."

    B. "It would be enjoyable to go to lunch with you all, but today I get to pick up my princess and take her to the park to play. We are going on big adventures!"

Side by side, there is a vast world between these two statements.

After making the first one, I felt stuck. How I wished to go and hang out with the boys. But unfortunately it was my day to go pick up the kid.

After rephrasing and making the second statement though, all the sudden I was the man! Simply changing the phrase "I've got to," into "I get to" will make a tremendous difference in your world. After rephrasing my statement, I actually felt better and thought, "Oh my God, it worked!"

Now instead of wishing to hang with the boys, I had chosen my daughter. It was my day to pick her up from kindergarten and I decided right then and there that we were going to have an amazing time playing together.

And we did.

The first statement is just a disaster; "I wish I could but I can't because I've got to do something else (that I don't really want to do)." as opposed to, "Too bad for you guys, but I get to do great things today!"

It is of the utmost importance that we pay attention and listen to what we are saying, because our word is the law. Our word is exactly how things are and how things shall be.

I can report that "getting to" is a lot more fun than "having to."

Affirmations

Affirmations are something that I'd seen a thousand times, but honestly admit that I didn't understand them. As OSHO points out, I didn't really believe them. This is not how I really felt, and initially I didn't see any reason to bother with this.

> *"If you are making positive affirmations it is because you don't believe them. Someone who is happy does not walk around repeating, "I am so happy! Look how happy I am!"*
> **OSHO**

Who wants to affirm that, "My life is filled with abundance!" while the bank account is near zero? It didn't make sense to me to affirm, "I am healthy and whole," when in reality I was sick.

Yet everywhere I turned, someone was suggesting that I use affirmations.

The book by Paramahansa Yogananda called "Scientific Healing Affirmations" seemed to speak to me, and it is of course, filled with statements of affirmations.

Then there was the Louise Hay book, "You Can Heal Yourself" which again, is filled with affirmative statements. Louise not only suggests using affirmations, but she speaks often about speaking them while looking into a mirror.

Then my wife and I began going to Unity, and once again I was met by this idea of positive affirmation.

It was quite obvious to me that this was what people were doing to change their lives, and so I began my own journey with them.

Now I understand them to work like this; we don't believe them or feel that way but we know that they are true. So it must be worked out within.

An example of this that I tell regularly is of me saying, "I am broke." I was on the phone with a friend one night and I was very upset, because my money situation was not exactly going the way I wanted.

I was really worked up into a frenzy.

My friend asked me, "What did you have for dinner?" and I told him that we had cooked hamburgers and had sat outside and ate those along with some watermelon.

"Where is your wife?" he asked. "In the living room watching TV." I told him.

"Your daughter?" "Oh she is asleep now." I said.

He asked me, "And where are you right now?" "I'm outside on the back porch." I said. But by now, I was starting to get the picture.

My friend was obviously pointing out to me that nothing was wrong, except for the fact that I had convinced myself that something was terribly wrong.

I'd had a wonderful dinner with my family, given my daughter a bath and read to her for story time. My wife was watching her TV shows, I was on the back patio, and there was really nothing wrong.

You see? Everyone is fed. We are at our own house. Our cars are both running.

So I saw that even though everything was okay, I had convinced myself otherwise. I saw that in all actuality I could be celebrating right now!

This experience taught me how to, "Talk myself down from the tree." This taught me that whenever I get really upset and worried, and I know that there is something wrong I need to simply sit down and assess the situation.

I don't have to do this so much anymore but have practiced it thousands of times, and can tell you that one-hundred percent of the time, nothing was wrong.

"I have eaten." "My family is clothed and fed." "We are here at our house."

As Master Eckhart Tolle says, "Acknowledging the good that you already have in your life is the foundation for all abundance."

My friend, along with Master Tolle also taught me, "There is never anything wrong right now."

And so I began to see that I was in fact, not broke at all. Even though this is the way I felt, it was not true. I saw the truth that everything was okay, and was able to begin to affirm that positive, instead of the old negative that I was so used to affirming.

And behold, my life began to get very different.

Every Sunday our minister at Unity has a routine in which he makes statements and we respond.

Minister: "The Light of God surrounds me."
Congregation: "I Am the Light of God!"
Minister: "The Love of God enfolds me."
Congregation; "I Am the Love of God!"
Minister: "The Power of God protects me."
Congregation; "I Am the Power of God!"
Minister: "The Presence of God watches over me."
Congregation: "I Am the Presence of God!"

Having been raised in a fundamental Christian church, I couldn't help but fear that we might get struck by lightning.

As my wife and I went back every Sunday, I began to find myself thinking about this during the week. What did I really think about this? Did this make sense to me? How did this feel? True, it felt a little uncomfortable, but had I not felt uncomfortable in the fundamental church? Had I not left the fundamental church at a very early age for certain reasons?

The result I concluded was to let go of my hesitations, and sort of make the responses under my breath.

Just to see what would happen.

After several months, one day I found myself loudly proclaiming them and feeling as if, "Hey, there might be something to this."

Several years later I found myself on the speaking circuit, leading large congregations through this exact series of affirmations that I'd learned from my Unity minister.

And this is how affirmations work for me. I start off with hesitation, feeling as if I'm not telling the truth. But I continue on and work through them, reminding myself that "this is the Truth."

At some point there is a moment when you go from trying to convince yourself, and you move into knowing.

This is when the affirmation becomes you. This is when you see things differently than before. This is when your life begins to reflect this new part of you.

There is reasoning involved.

The trick to reasoning is that you can make a case for anything. We have to decide if we want to stick with what we have, or if a positive outlook would provide us a better reality.

Re-Framing
It is our perception of a person, a situation, or a past event, that has created the inner associations that we carry around and which make us up.

I have worked with people who have had terrible problems with their weight, with people who had terrible problems with alcohol and drugs, gambling, all sorts of problems and addictions.

"A miracle is a shift in perception."
Marianne Williamson

I have also worked with people who have experienced trauma and loss, and those who have suffered abuse of all kinds.

There comes a time for us, no matter the intensity of the situation or how "bad" the situation may be, when we have to conclude that "If there is a problem, there has to be a solution."

When something is affecting us in a negative way and creating life in ways that we don't want, it is time to find the solution.

One of the fundamental things for us to understand is that the pain really is necessary.

Pain is the indicator. Pain lets us know that something is wrong.

In every case, this pain is all that we know. Sometimes we get some kind of glory out of pain. We can become a martyr, even if only to ourselves. We carry the pain as if it was a flag. It can become our identity and how we see ourselves. It is definitely the story that we tell ourselves about ourselves. And so it is difficult to let go of the pain and move into the unknown. When we reach that point where the pain is intolerable anymore, it is time to change our perception.

And to change our perception is the only way. We must put down the flag and change this story that we have been telling ourselves about ourselves.

We cannot rewind back in time and change what has happened, but what we can change is our perception and response.

We are responding according to our perception. When we are troubled, it is because we are responding with negative life patterns.

Often in my own case it was as if I said, "Well since you did this thing that hurt me, I will now hurt myself more and continue to do so every day!" I would take a bad situation or circumstance and respond by making it worse.

This is as insane as it sounds, but look at yourself and look around and you will see that this is a normal human behavior pattern.

When we realize that we aren't hurting anyone but ourselves, we will want to change. Most of the time the people that we are angry at and hurt by aren't even in the picture anymore. And yet still we hurt ourselves and cannot seem to stop.

And we can agree that this is an inappropriate response.

Once we can agree on this, we are halfway to freedom! There is no reason to excuse bad or abusive behavior; there is no reason to say that it was okay for someone to hurt us.

In other words, we don't have to say that what someone else may have said or done was right or good, what we have to do is more closely examine the situation and our response to the situation.

What we have done is we have taken a bad situation and we have made it worse. In every case we have taken something personally that was in no way personal.

I always refer back to the book "The Four Agreements" by Don Miguel Ruiz, because in this book we are taught that nothing is personal. We are taught that it is impossible for a person to say or do anything to anyone that isn't about themselves. When we lash out in any way, we are lashing out at our own selves.
A person who has the need to lash out does not feel very good inside to begin with. There is pain inside, and so they are simply bringing the pain into physical form.

I have come to look at people and their lives and what they say and do as if it is all a painting. "Look what is inside of me" is what we are saying.

People are showing us what is inside them, and we are doing the same.

Once while working with a client who had been terribly abused during her childhood, I witnessed a tremendous awakening. "Oh my God that poor man!" she exclaimed. "I never realized how bad he must have felt inside."

Now she cried, but instead of crying over what the man had done to her, she was crying because she realized that his behavior had nothing to do with her. She was crying because she saw that what he had done was simply show his pain. And since the outer world is a reflection of the inner world, then what else can a person do? She made two statements that I clearly remember. The first was, "That poor man!" and the second was, "I always thought that I was responsible!" To describe the change that came over this woman while we were sitting there would be impossible.

She changed.

It was a different woman leaving than the one who had walked in. I didn't see her again for nearly a year and when we met again I hardly recognized her.

Many of the difficulties that she'd had in life had slipped away and she had the biggest smile on her face. What happened was that this woman found a different way to look at her life. She let go of the old, and took on a different perception of a situation.

The rest happened accordingly.

There have been times in my life while working with our technique that I have simply said to the Universe, "I need a new story!" or "How can I see this in a different way?" When something isn't going the way I want, it can only be because my perception has created this story.

When the story changes, then your life will change.

Chapter ten questions:

1. I now am going to give you the project of finding positive affirmations that fit your situation. Find three or four good affirmations that resonate with you, and work with them every day for a while. Spend ten to twenty minutes each day speaking the affirmations, and exploring how you feel about them. I have printed affirmations out and taped them to the mirror where I get dressed in the morning, and even on the dashboard of my car. Place them where you will see them several times a day.

    You must convince yourself that they are true, and when that happens, the affirmations will appear in physical form in your life.

2. Begin paying close attention to what you say. Listen to yourself. Remember that what you say will be how things are. Remember how powerful your words are. What are some things that you say regularly that you might need to change? And what will you say instead? Write these out and say them out loud to get used to them, and then make a commitment to begin using them in conversation.

    Re-framing is a very important process for us all. Is there something that you just cannot seem to get over? Is there something or someone that you cannot forgive? Has something bad happened to you in the past that still has a negative impact on you today? Is there any way for you to find a positive way to look at it? If you need help with this, please seek help, because remember, you were suffering then, and you continue to suffer. There is no need to suffer for a lifetime over a single person or incident, no matter what it was. Free yourself.

Chapter Eleven
The Most Subtle Thought

"When your inner world comes into order, your outer world will come into order."
I Ching

What you will undoubtedly find most fascinating about using this technique and doing your inner work, is that when the inner work is done, the outer will just change. Though you have used the technique, dedicated yourself to change, and done the work, when you see the results they will surprise you.

Because none of the work is actually done on the outside.

It used to be that I had the filthiest mouth imaginable. I'd battled with alcoholism and drug addictions, worked with construction crews, and this was just the way we all spoke to one another.

There was a time when I thought, "Maybe I should try to do something about this." but honestly, my language was so bad, that the idea seemed silly. When something is that far gone, there is no use. It would be impossible. I can remember having these thoughts and then just disregarding it altogether.

Until one morning when I awoke to find that my language had been cleaned up.

It happened during an early morning phone call. Each time I went to speak a curse word, a different word came out. Words like "darn," "frigging," and "heck" began to sneak in front of the curse words. This took me a little by surprise, but throughout the day I noticed that the pattern continued.

After several days had gone by I said to a friend of mine, "Something very strange has happened." He asked me what it was that had happened, and I explained what had been going on. He told me that he had noticed, and that it had been obvious. He had decided to not say anything and wait until I brought it up.

We both marveled at the change, and at how to me it seemed as if I wasn't doing it. I'd never meant to change my language in the least. We are talking about pretty much a lifetime of constant cursing that changed instantly and with no effort on my part. I remembered having thought about the cursing and disregarding the idea of trying to clean up my language. But I had totally dismissed it and hadn't thought anymore about it. Could a thought this simple and small, just a passing thought, really have this kind of impact?

Yes.

And the truth is that all of our thoughts have this exact same kind of impact.

Everything about us has this same kind of impact, and this is how our lives are formed. By us.

Chapter Twelve
The Responsibility Clause

"If you suffer it is because of you, if you feel blissful it is because of you. Nobody else is responsible – only you and you alone. You are your hell and your heaven too."
OSHO

There was certainly a time when I was totally unaware of all of this information.

I spent many years unaware of my "true self" or my "Presence." I thought that I was my thoughts. My mentality was totally that of a victim. During this time, other people and circumstances were responsible for me.

I wasn't.

After all, I would not have done what I did unless you did what you did. "Look what you made me do!" "You made me angry!"

There is a joke that goes around at times; "It isn't my fault that you made me push you down the stairs!" The insanity of this idea is quite obvious, but in all honesty, this was exactly the way I thought while living in victim consciousness.

What I did was your fault.

But one day it became clear that though I was pointing fingers outward at everyone and everything else, I was the one who was paying the price.

It was me who was going backwards in life instead of forward. It was me who had lots of problems and couldn't figure out how to overcome them. It was me who was living a life in which nothing was the way I wanted it to be.

It was me who felt bad.

There is no chance for us until we make the transition from victim consciousness to God Consciousness.

This requires deciding and realizing that it is I who am responsible for my thoughts, feelings, and actions.

As long as it is someone else's fault, then they have the power. And we have given them this power.

Under these circumstances it was as if God put me here on earth in this body, and it was torture. I was not enjoying living. There were too many troubles and they kept piling up. I was trapped and could not move forward. And to make matters worse, when I tried to move forward it seemed to only set me back further.

It seemed as if the world and everyone in it was against me, and I couldn't do anything about it. And this is pure victim mentality.

At first I could only entertain the idea of the possibility that it was me who was responsible for my thoughts, feelings, and actions. But as time went on and I awoke to the true reality, my life began to change and I could clearly see it as it happened.

It turns out that I do have power over my thoughts. Yes it took work and practice, but I can in fact, decide what to think about. It turns out that no matter what you say or do, it is for me to decide how I will respond.

It turns out also, that the realization that I do have power after all, feels really good. When this change happens to a person it is tremendous. This is a complete and total psychic change. In most cases it is a change that takes time.

It is a great transition to take back our power.

Once it has begun, it is up to us to remain steadfast in continuing and making sure we are doing our inner work.

The communication lines between you and the Universe are wide open and functioning properly.

The Universe is communicating with you now and it always has been.

Likewise, you are communicating to the Universe and you always have been.

When our lives are not as we wish, it is not because the Universe is having problems, it is because of the signals that we are sending/communicating to the Universe.

The Universe responds to you perfectly as you instruct it. The Universe can only do what you tell it to do.

It can only be what you are.

The outer world around you is a movie, and you are the projector.

This means that we must accept 100% responsibility for our lives. This technique described in this book and spiritual growth in general, depends entirely upon acceptance and the understanding of this knowledge.

In other words, if there is a problem, it cannot be with the Universe. It can only be within us.

We must know that whatever is in our outer world, is simply being projected by the inner world.

This means being able to say, "If it is in my life, I am the one who put it there".

Take Back Your Power
When clients come to see me and we are having our initial sit down talk, I always first need to know the reason for their visit. "So what's going on with you?" I ask. This is a nice polite invitation for them to let it all out.

I just want people to talk, because the more they talk, the more I can listen. I listen for emotion, and I listen for what they don't say. I watch and observe them too, looking at body language, observing the looks on their faces, and I may ask a question here and there just to clarify something, but I try to stay quiet.

Not always, but usually it pours out of them like a flood, all the things that are bothering them, and usually a long list of problems arises.

They've been cheated on by a lover or spouse, they are having anger problems at work, they are so stressed that they cannot go to work or function the way they would like, they are suffering from migraines or some other physical issue.

Sometimes they want to quit drinking or smoking, or they want to lose weight.

Others are working towards an objective and finding it seemingly next to impossible.

> *"I am not what happened to me. I am what I chose to become."*
> ## *Carl Jung*

There are those who were abused while growing up, there are those who have lost children, and there are those who have had a traumatic experience.

Sometimes they were victim, and sometimes they were to blame.

It is my job to sort things out and then present a simplified outline of what is going on, back to the client. I identify "This is what you want", and "This is what is in the way".

What we identify as "in the way" is then labeled as the main issues or problem(s).

These are the things we must overcome, in order to get our desired result or intention.

Typically people have a glaring problem that stands out. It is the one biggie that they can't seem to get a handle on, such as losing weight, or winning the battle with alcohol, or they have had a long string of unhealthy relationships and now they are in yet another one.

It seems to us as if our failure in life is caused by someone else or it is caused by a circumstance. In other words, it isn't our fault.

This causes us to look at our lives and think that is not a reflection of ourselves, but it is the reflection of what others have said or done, or that it is the reflection of our circumstance.

In living in this way, we have given away all of our power.

And not only have we given away our power, when we blame our lives on another person or circumstance, we are in essence being dishonest.

Your life is not someone else's fault.

But as long as you say that it is someone else's fault, then it will be. And the Universe will keep on responding to that command. You will keep getting the same things as always, because you are in a repetitive cycle.

Truth be told, we don't know any better at the time. When we are children we don't necessarily know how to deal with an abusive parent. Later in life we may not know how to deal with unfortunate circumstances.

I go through this process with the client thoroughly, because everything must be straight and clear and out on the table. Often times they have had so many things rambling through their mind, they are now refreshed to have a simple picture.

It is at this point that I begin the journey of explaining to them that what we have identified as their "problem" is not the problem at all.

It couldn't possibly be. We think that this thing or person that we have identified as the "problem" is what is keeping us from getting what we want; we think this is the problem. I have to agree that our "problem" is in the way, but it is for me to gently explain that what we have identified as the problem is an effect, and not a cause.

We think that "food" is our problem, or "alcohol" is our problem, and we blame our bad relationships or problems at work on other people. We spend all our time and energy on what we perceive to be the problem. We go on countless diets, we try to have more "self control", we really do try and we really do try hard. We exert all our will power, but in the end, we are right back where we started.

Think about it. Food doesn't fly off the grocery store shelf and into your mouth.

Alcohol doesn't just magically drift into your hand, and your credit cards do not fly out of your wallet and buy things that you cannot afford.

When it comes to other people, they can only be in our lives if we decide to allow them to be, and they can only treat us how we allow.

Even in unfortunate situations in which people force themselves upon us or in to our lives, it is for us to decide how we will respond.

Are we going to respond to a negative with a negative? Or are we going to search for a positive approach?

Are we going to rise above? Or are we going to let one isolated incident ruin the entire rest of our lives?

Are we going to give away our power? Or are we going to accept and use our power?

Are we going to continue to live under false pretense? Or are we ready now to live in Truth?

The responsibility clause is in no way to cast blame or to point fingers at ourselves. This is about a realization. This is about a Spiritual Awakening to the Truth and to the Power that we are each blessed with.

We Are Not Responsible For Other People

When we own up and take responsibility for our lives, we at the same time, release any ideas that we are responsible for other people. When I was filled with blame and excuses, I was also very sure that I was responsible for what other people had said and done.

How could I be responsible for things that an adult had said or done to me when I was a child? How can I be responsible for anyone now?

No child is responsible for what any adult does. No adult is responsible for what any other adult does. Each individual is responsible for his or her own self.
We never take responsibility for what someone else has said or done.

When someone has done wrong, we don't say that what they did was right, but we must now take responsibility for how we have responded. Or else we are saying that our lives are someone else's responsibility.

In other words we might say that, "I am the way I am because of what he did."

But we cannot do this.

We must be able to go a bit deeper and say, "I am the way I am because this is how I decided to respond to what he did."

This is a very different response to say, "I decided to respond this way."
This is when we take back our power.

We are taking back our power because if we decided to respond in a certain way, then we are free at any time to decide to respond a different way.

Now our power is not in the hands of someone else or some life circumstance.

Our power is in our hands.

A most beautiful thing happens here because when I realized that I could only experience my own vibrations, it occurred to me that the same is true for everyone else.

You can only experience your vibrations. And what you think and how you feel and what you do, is not my responsibility. In the same way that you are not responsible for me, I am not responsible for you.

The Truth
Once we take away the "outer" as being the actual problem, a person usually has no idea whatsoever what is causing their problem.

When we are at least willing to entertain the idea that our lives are our responsibility, and that everything in our lives is a reflection from within, we can make great progress.

The moment we begin to realize that it wasn't what the other person said or did, but how we responded to it, is the moment that our great change begins.

Now we can use the technique in this book and not only discover the true cause, we can also discover how to remove it.

Now if we so choose, we can give a command to the Universe such as, "Show me how to respond to this in a positive way!"

And the Universe will make this known to you.

This is how we remove a blockage. We turn negative energy (blockage) into positive energy (open).

This is where we acknowledge our power and decide to use it.

We decide to respond positively.

We take responsibility and in doing this we enter into the realm of Truth.

Entering the realm of Truth will find us bring our vibration into alignment with the Universe.

And this is the moment that we will begin to experience the sensation of "Oneness," and this is what each of us has truly been longing for all this time.

Chapter twelve questions:

1. Who and what have you blamed your life on? Was it a person or was it a circumstance?

2. Are you prepared to take full responsibility for your life? Or are there still some things that you blame on other people?

3. Can you see how in making other people responsible for your life, you have given up your power? Write about these situations and show how you were wrong. Write about how it will be now that you have taken back your power.

4. Are there people in which you feel responsible for? People who tell you that you make them feel a certain way or that you made them do a certain thing?

5. Are you prepared to deny now that you are responsible for another person's thoughts, feelings, and actions?

Chapter Thirteen
The Thing We Want The Most

"Our deepest fear is not that we are inadequate. Our deepest fear is that we are powerful beyond measure. It is our Light, not our Darkness, that most frightens us."
Marianne Williamson

During the course of this book we have established that we are the ones who are responsible for our lives.

We have also established that we have access to the ability to change.

But it is as if there are two of us. There is a part of us that wants to change, that wishes to change, and then there is the part that resists.

When it comes to changing behavior, there is nobody standing there who won't let you. Our obsession, the thing that we think about all the time, that thing we say we so badly desire, can only be kept from us by us.

"Why don't you just have one drink instead of ten?" "Why don't you just handle your money better?" "Why don't you just stop the negative behavior?"

It turns out that what we want to change, or what we want to attract into our lives the most, is the thing that we are most afraid of.

My negative behaviors are what I know as "me." This is how I associate with myself. This is what makes up my self-image. They do something for me. And it is as if I want to act as a child and say, "No! This is mine!"

And we hold on for dear life.

Behind this there can be hidden many deeper aspects of our psyche. We can feel unworthy, we can be afraid to fail, we can be afraid that if we change we might lose people who are in our lives.

We walk around saying, "I want this" over and over, sometimes for years. But we cannot give it to ourselves.

For years as a musician, I longed for a lot more success than I ever got. When I used the technique in this book to explore what had been going on,

I found things that amazed me.

Being a recovering addict, there was a fear of what would happen if suddenly I had the money to do whatever I wanted. How would I react? Would I stay clean?

Success would also change the dynamics of my relationship with my wife? How would she react if our options changed?

Then there is the pressure. There is the pressure of being in front of lots of people. There is pressure because you are on a pedestal, like it or not.

Today as the spiritual leader of my own church I'd like for the church to grow, but there is the pressure of having to deal with all the personalities.

Some people get mad at me and leave the church. Some people from other churches ridicule me or question me. What if I say the wrong thing? What if things don't go according to plan?

Using the technique you are going to find out exactly the thoughts that are keeping you where you are, and you will see that they are all fear based.

So then I want to be successful, but success is the thing I am most afraid of. You want to quit smoking, but quitting is the thing you are most afraid of. You want to lose weight, but this is the thing you are most afraid of. You want to be in a healthy relationship but this is what you are most afraid of.

We can instruct the Universe to, "Tell me what it is that I am afraid of." or "Why am I afraid to be successful?"

Soon what you fear will be brought to you. We must face our fears in order to overcome them. This is the only way.

Several years ago I was a part of a concert in Charlotte NC. Everything was all fine and normal until the minute before I was to take the stage.

My heart raced and my hands trembles uncontrollably.

"What is going on?" I thought. This was a concert and I have given a thousand concerts and there is nothing here out of the ordinary at all. I'm about to go on stage and do the same thing I've done over and over, and so what is the trouble here?

But still the nervousness tried to take me. It was really bad, and I thought I might faint.

Yet I somehow knew what it was. I knew it was fear and I knew that though it was real fear, there was in all actuality nothing to be afraid of. After all, there was nothing out of the ordinary.

I said to myself, "I am going to walk out there and play, even if I forget the words and mess up every note on the guitar."

I said to my fear, "You will not win."

It was as if I was fighting with myself as I started the song. The hands shook; it was pretty rocky at first.

But then the fear realized that I was going to do it either way. Before long the fear and anxiety had left me and I was playing and singing my heart out like never before.

Why did my fear choose this night? Why now? This I still don't know, but from time to time, I am confronted with situations like this, and when they come, I give it my all to not back down.

But sometimes in life, we are all overcome with fear.

Though there are times when I face and overcome fears, there are also times when the fear is too much for me and I stay put.

The process reminds me that when a man has been in darkness for a long time in that you cannot just take his blindfold off in the sun, because this will blind him.

His eyes must be given time to adjust slowly to the light.

Always remember that this is a process. We practice, we grow, and we evolve. We must take it easy on ourselves and know that if we cannot do it today or "yet" that the day will come when we will do it.

Having faith does not mean that we aren't afraid it means that we do it anyway.

As we awaken to the Universe and learn that it is not against us, we can let more and more of our fears slip away.

Let there be no more excuses standing between us, and the life we want to live.

Be the light that you are.

Chapter thirteen questions:

1. Have you ever let fear keep you from doing something that you really wanted to do? Write about that.

2. Have you ever done something even though you were afraid? How did you feel afterwards? Write about this experience.

3. We need to understand that to have faith does not mean that we aren't afraid. Having faith means that we do it anyway even if we are feeling fear. If there is something that you want to do but are afraid to do, write about it. See that there is no reason to fear and that any fear is unfounded. Make the case for this and make the decision that "I will do it anyway!"

Chapter Fourteen
And So It Already Is!

Today it feels as if I must be the luckiest man alive.

The cicadas are singing, my wife is at work in her home-office, while my daughter is watching television and waiting on one of her friends to arrive.

It is a hot day here in Georgia, just the way I like it. I feel pleased.

It turns out that a person can be miserable in any situation. Or a person can be happy in any situation.

This is for each person to decide.

My happiness has absolutely nothing to do with any situation or life circumstance, and neither did the unhappiness that was my life for so long.

Happiness and unhappiness do not come from other people or from material things.

Our happiness or our unhappiness, along with everything and everyone that is in our lives, comes from within us.

So if we want to change, it is within that we must go.

I've done my best to describe and lay out for you the experiences and the process that I've gone through over the years.

Using the technique, you can discover what the problem is, where the problem is, and also, how to erase the problem or better yet, change the vibration.

I have witnessed actual physical healings. I have seen people change appearances before my eyes.

I have seen people get the better job, discover their true selves, become happy in their relationships, become free of negative life patterns and addictions, and I have watched as people create the lives that they have always wanted.

As I sit here nearing the end of my first book, it occurs to me that on the outside, not much has really changed. I still have the same daughter and wife, and we still live in the same house we have lived in for over ten years now.

It is true that instead of playing music in bars every night, I am now a music director for a church, and I do travel giving talks and playing music at other churches. I still play music but in different places.

It is also true that a Spiritual Community has grown around me, and I am the Spiritual Leader of my own church.

My finances are better. My health is better.

But mostly what has happened is that I have gone from living in my perceived "Hell" most of the time, to living in my perceived "Heaven" most of the time.

I changed my perception and my story. I used the technique described in this book to find out what negative vibrations were causing negativity in my life, and I faced them and I changed them.

I urge you to remember at all times that we are moving. Life is a process and a transition.

There will always be things that you would like to change or make better. We will always be in the process of growing.

You will set goals and intentions and you will accomplish them. And then when you do, you will set more.

But at any given time along this path, you are okay right here and now.

One day you will trust and have so much faith in the Universe that you will even let all of your goals and intentions go. You will deeply understand that your only purpose is to be you.

You will one day know that you are good. You are of God. You were created by Creator just as you are.
When this great realization comes to you, and it shall, you will "just be."

And we will see one another and know.

This is how it has been for me. When I open my eyes now, I don't see the same things and people I used to see. Even though they are for the most part the very same things and people.

When I look in the mirror, I don't see the same person there either.

When I look outward through my eyes, I only see God. When I look into the mirror at myself and within myself, I only see God.

Everything is different now, and everything is Heavenly now. Everything is God now.

And it is nice living in Heaven.

"I bow to Creator and I bow to all of Creation.
God is All and All is God.
I see God in all people and in all things.
I see God as You
And I see God as me.
And so it already is."

Chapter fourteen questions:

1. If we have been placing our focus on things and people that we are grateful for our lives will already have become more fruitful. We will already have more things and people that we want in our lives. How has your life changed since the beginning of this workbook?

2. Write about your experiences with the Universal Laws and how you have learned to work in accord with them now.

3. Because you now have taken back your power of responsibility, realized your true power to get any information you may need from the Universe, you can now do anything you want. Write about not what you want to do, but about what you are doing. Write about not how you would like your life to become, but about how your life is already becoming.

4. Remember our prayer and recite it often;

"I bow to Creator and I bow to all of Creation.
God is All and All is God.
I see God in all people and in all things.
I see God as You
And I see God as me.
And so it already is."

Appendix
Chapter Questions

Chapter two questions:

1. After reading through this book, now it is time for you to make your command. It is time to state what you want, what you want to change, or what you want to know.

   I invite you to write it out on paper, but also say it aloud. Feel good now and "know that you know." Release it.

2. Now I invite you to sit down and make a list of all the things and people that are in your life that you like.

   What I am searching for here is to find out what you like about your life.

   Often our focus is so strongly attached to our puzzle and what we don't like, that it may be difficult to steer your mind away from it.

   But steering the mind away is what we will have to do if we want this technique to work. Knowing that we know, we will make our request/command and then we must leave it alone.

   We must learn to put our focus elsewhere, thus the list of things that we like in our lives.

   Once we have this list, then any time we catch ourselves obsessing over the puzzle, we can re-direct ourselves onto something positive from our list.

3. What are some ways that I can place more focus on the people that I care about? Can I call them? Send a card? What nice things can I do to nurture these relationships?

4. What are some ways that I can focus on things that I like in my life? Have I been taking any free time for enjoyment or hobbies? Can I get involved in a project around the yard or the house?

Get busy and stay busy with your focus on the people and things that you are grateful for.

Chapter three questions:

1. Looking back on your life, how would you imagine your past associations? Would you think that you would have more negative associations than positive?

2. Have you ever experienced something that took you back in time? You could have smelled a familiar smell, tasted a familiar food, or run across someone from your past. The moment you encounter something or someone from the past, your brain brings up the associations, and suddenly you feel exactly like you did in the past.

3. Write about your general disposition. Do you see yourself as a positive "glass half full" kind of person? Or are you the opposite?

4. Would you say that you look for the good in things and speak positively?

Chapter four questions:

1. How do you truly feel about the idea of Universal Consciousness?

2. Have you ever tapped into the Universal Consciousness, or known anyone who did?

Chapter five questions:

1. Are you a person who has never tried? Why?

2. Are you a person who has tried and failed? Write about yourself and how you see yourself. Why do you think you failed? Are you ready to try again? Or to make a go at something else?

3. Everyone has something or a few things that they would love to do, but are convinced that these things would be impossible. Things like scuba-diving, travel to exotic locations, parachuting out of an airplane, or starting your own business. Whatever the desire may be, we have reasons why we cannot actually do what we would like to do.

    Write about your "impossible dream or dreams."

4. How can you use our technique, to help you accomplish your

"impossible dream?" What are some commands you could give? What do you need to know?

5. I am going to invite you now to choose an "impossible dream," and use the technique in this book to help you achieve it. Get a journal or notebook specifically for this adventure. And send me pictures of yourself living your "impossible dream!"

Chapter six questions:

1. With the things you want to change about yourself or with the things you would like to do, can you see how you have made it all personal?

2. How have you been out of line with Universal Laws?

3. Write out and make a case for what you want, and show how it is not personal. What Universal Laws can you use, and how can you bring yourself more in line with the Laws?

Chapter eight questions:

1. In past endeavors, have you had extreme thinking? Have you tried to go from A to Z without all the steps in between?

2. Writing out your current goals and intentions, draw a map that includes all the steps necessary to achieve your goal. Create a pathway from where you are to where you want to go.

3. Now take that first step!

Chapter nine questions:

1. If there is a puzzle that you have had for a long time, we know that you have been giving the wrong command, or asking the wrong question. Thus we have to change the command or the question. Now we ask questions like, "What is blocking me from this?" or "What is truly causing this?"

2. Often what the Universe shows us is going to be painful. We must remember that the cause is negative associations in the brain. Once you make the command, the Universe will bring it to you and show you. Are you prepared to deal with painful situations from your past?

3. Are there situations that come to mind that you are not prepared to deal with?

4. Remember that you can also use this technique to command, "Show me how to heal from this." Once again, the Universe has no choice but to show you. Whatever the case, the negative associations can be turned into positive.

5. Look for mixed messages. Do you say one thing one minute, but then rebuke it in some way the next? Are you saying that you want something, but then not making any changes in your life or moves towards what you say you want? Write about how you can be more harmonious and stop sending mixed messages.

Chapter ten questions:

1. I now am going to give you the project of finding positive affirmations that fit your situation. Find three or four good affirmations that resonate with you, and work with them every day for a while. Spend ten to twenty minutes each day speaking the affirmations, and exploring how you feel about them. I have printed affirmations out and taped them to the mirror where I get dressed in the morning, and even on the dashboard of my car. Place them where you will see them several times a day.

    You must convince yourself that they are true, and when that happens, the affirmations will appear in physical form in your life.

2. Begin paying close attention to what you say. Listen to yourself. Remember that what you say will be how things are. Remember how powerful your words are. What are some things that you say regularly that you might need to change? And what will you say instead? Write these out and say them out loud to get used to them, and then make a commitment to begin using them in conversation.

3. Re-framing is a very important process for us all. Is there something that you just cannot seem to get over? Is there something or someone that you cannot forgive? Has something bad happened to you in the past that still has a negative impact on you today? Is there any way for you to find a positive way to look at it? If you need help with this, please seek help, because remember, you were suffering then, and you continue to suffer. There is no need to suffer for a lifetime over a single person or incident, no matter what it was. Free yourself.

Chapter twelve questions:

1. Who and what have you blamed your life on? Was it a person or was it a circumstance?

2. Are you prepared to take full responsibility for your life? Or are there still some things that you blame on other people?

3. Can you see how in making other people responsible for your life, you have given up your power? Write about these situations and show how you were wrong. Write about how it will be now that you have taken back your power.

4. Are there people in which you feel responsible for? People who tell you that you make them feel a certain way or that you made them do a certain thing?

5. Are you prepared to deny now that you are responsible for another person's thoughts, feelings, and actions?

Chapter thirteen questions:

1. Have you ever let fear keep you from doing something that you really wanted to do? Write about that.

2. Have you ever done something even though you were afraid? How did you feel afterwards? Write about this experience.

3. We need to understand that to have faith does not mean that we aren't afraid. Having faith means that we do it anyway even if we are feeling fear. If there is something that you want to do but are afraid to do, write about it. See that there is no reason to fear and that any fear is unfounded. Make the case for this and make the decision that "I will do it anyway!"

Chapter fourteen questions:

1. If we have been placing our focus on things and people that we are grateful for our lives will already have become more fruitful. We will already have more things and people that we want in our lives. How has your life changed since the beginning of this workbook?

2. Write about your experiences with the Universal Laws and how you have learned to work in accord with them now.

3. Because you now have taken back your power of responsibility, realized your true power to get any information you may need from the Universe, you can now do anything you want. Write about not what you want to do, but about what you are doing. Write about not how you would like your life to become, but about how your life is already becoming.

4. Remember our prayer and recite it often;

"I bow to Creator and I bow to all of Creation.
God is All and All is God.
I see God in all people and in all things.
I see God as You
And I see God as me.
And so it already is."

About the Author

Kyle Shiver is the visionary and founder of Spirit Ministries and Spiritual Leader at Tybee Spirit, and New Though spiritual community on Tybee Island Georgia.

Kyle has a bachelor degree in Spiritual Healing from the Yogananda Institute, and is certified in life coaching, reiki, chakra balancing, and meditation.

Kyle is also music director at Unity of Savannah, and travels to Unity church's in the southeast playing music, giving talks, and leading workshops. He is currently studying to become a Licensed Unity Teacher.

For spiritual counsel and healing sessions via phone or Skype, or to schedule Kyle to come to your church or healing center, please call 912-604-3762 or e-mail kyleshiver@me.com.

www.spiritministries.net   www.tybeespirit.org

Made in the USA
Charleston, SC
31 August 2015